C. S. Lewis:
Clarity and Confusion

A balanced introduction to his writings

DayOne

© Day One Publications 2006

First printed 2006

ISBN: 978-1-84625-046-0

9 781846 250460

British Library Cataloguing in Publication Data available

Published by Day One Publications
Ryelands Road, Leominster, HR6 8NZ
☎ 01568 613 740 FAX 01568 611 473
email—sales@dayone.co.uk
web site—www.dayone.co.uk
North American—e-mail—sales@dayonebookstore.com
North American—web site—www.dayonebookstore.com

Designed by Steve Devane and printed by Gutenberg Press, Malta

Contents

Commendations

Andrew Wheeler displays a great depth and breadth of understanding of Lewis's writings with respect to the Christian faith; the quotations, sources and related biblical references are extremely thorough and helpful. The book is an enlightened journey through Lewis's thoughts and insights as expressed in his letters and popular writing. It is very useful as an introduction to Lewis in general and also as a cautionary note to those who already love his legacy of Christian literature but may need challenging to reflect more carefully where he deviates from the more orthodox evangelical understanding of biblical truth.

Andrew Wheeler commends and endorses Lewis where his writings conform to orthodox evangelical theology and takes issue with him when they do not. He does so in a scholarly and confrontational manner with which Lewis would have engaged with relish. Lewis loved a good argument. The frequently used practice in the book of first outlining biblical teaching on a topic and then setting Lewis's writings against that template is a useful device that works well—I don't know of any other book that does this. It is worth bearing in mind that if at times the author comes across as self-opinionated he is not advancing a claim to superior powers of reasoning but rather an appeal to biblical truth.

—Dr Hadden Wilson, retired Pastor of Ballynahinch Baptist Church, Northern Ireland, currently part-time lecturer at Belfast Bible College and Adjunct Professor with John Brown University, Arkansas, USA

What are Evangelical Christians to make of C. S. Lewis? Lewis, an Ulsterman, lived a rich and varied life. He was an Oxford don, a veteran of the Western Front in the Great War, a lifelong bachelor whose late and brief marriage to the American Joy Gresham was the subject of the recent play, Shadowlands. His death occurred on the same day in 1963 as the assassination in Dallas of President John F. Kennedy. Raised with a conventional Church of Ireland upbringing, Lewis lost his faith while still at school and flirted with atheism for several years until a decisive conversion prepared the way for a surprising and fruitful new direction. Though not a theologian, this Anglican layman became an apologist for what he called 'Mere Christianity' through a series of popular books that continue to be best sellers, not least the famous Narnia stories for children. A minor industry of Lewis studies has grown up around his legacy. Nevertheless, most Evangelicals would agree that Lewis needs to be read with discernment. Andrew Wheeler has sifted through his writings with great care and provided us with a valuable guide that will help us get the best out of our reading. There is generous praise for Lewis the Christian communicator as well as judicious warnings for those areas where Evangelicals would part company with this gifted scholar and author.
—J. Phil Arthur, Pastor of Free Grace Baptist Church, Lancaster, England

This book is for
Ian and Mary,
Daniel, Hannah, Naomi, Sarah-Anne and Jonathan.
It was begun in their house.

Preface

Among evangelicals there are very different views of C. S. Lewis. At one end of the spectrum, there are those who think so highly of him that they hardly ever disagree with what he says. At the other end, there are those who do not regard him as a Christian at all.

The truth, I believe, is in between. I am completely certain that he was a Christian, but at the same time, his views on some matters are deeply troubling. The two main Parts of this book (Parts 2 and 3) reflect this twofold perspective. In Part 2 we look at God's grace at work in Lewis, because grace is always worth seeing. We can learn, too, from the truths which grace enabled him to express in writing. Part 3 deals with subjects where we should be wary of Lewis's views. We can benefit greatly from Lewis's books, but there are dangers in them too, and we need to be on guard against them. My hope and prayer is that this book will help us to do both.

Each chapter in Parts 2 and 3 ends with a small number of quotations from Lewis on the subject the chapter deals with. I got this idea from an excellent series of books on church history called *2,000 Years of Christ's Power*. For this reason I am grateful to the author of that series, Dr N. R. Needham, though I do not know him personally. I would also like to thank all those who made this book a subject of prayer while it was being written. Thanks especially to Steve Walker, whose old computer and printer have handled every word you're about to read, and Paul Brown, who kindly read some chapters in draft and made very helpful suggestions. In particular, a major improvement in chapter 4 is due to Paul.

Andrew Wheeler

1 A sketch of his life

Early years

Clive Staples Lewis was born on 29 November 1898 at his family's Belfast home. His father Albert was a solicitor, and his mother Florence (known as Flora) was the daughter of a Church of Ireland clergyman. They had one older son, Warren, born in 1895. The boys became known as Warnie and Jack, names that were used by family and friends for the rest of their lives. The family was fairly well off, but tragedy struck in 1908 when Flora Lewis died of cancer. Warnie and Jack were only thirteen and nine respectively.

Later that year Jack followed Warnie to boarding school in England. Their father had chosen Wynyard School at Watford in Hertfordshire, run by the Rev. Robert Capron. It was a disastrous choice. By the time the Lewis boys went there, the school was on its way downhill. Mr Capron was becoming more and more mentally unstable, and as a result, very cruel to his pupils. In 1910 the school closed. Capron was later certified insane and died in an asylum the following year.

For Jack, there followed a Belfast school, a lengthy illness, and then, in 1913, a very good preparatory school in Malvern, Worcestershire. Warnie was already at the public school there, Malvern College, and Jack followed in 1913. Here, for various reasons, he was again extremely unhappy. Public school life did not suit him at all. In spite of one outstanding teacher who he always remembered with affection, he asked his father to remove him. Perhaps surprisingly, Albert Lewis agreed, and in September 1914 Jack's education underwent a dramatic improvement.

Albert's old headmaster, W. T. Kirkpatrick, was now taking private pupils at his home in Great Bookham, Surrey. Over the previous year he had helped Warnie prepare to enter the Royal Military College, Sandhurst, where he trained as an army officer. Now he supervised Jack's education for the next two and a half years. Here Jack was very happy. His academic potential was enormous, and Mr Kirkpatrick must take most of the credit for developing his talents.

University and war

In December 1916 Jack was accepted by University College, Oxford. But this was in the middle of the First World War, and he was now old enough to serve in the army. As an Irishman he could have claimed exemption from this, but he decided to serve anyway. He joined the University Officers' Training Corps, and in June 1917 began training in earnest.

In his cadet battalion he began a friendship which was to have far-reaching consequences. E. F. C. Moore, known as Paddy, was a fellow Irishman and the same age as Jack. A strong bond developed between Jack and the whole Moore family: Paddy, his mother (who was separated from her husband), and his eleven-year-old sister Maureen.

At the end of September 1917 Jack was made a 2nd Lieutenant and given a month's leave from the army. His father was very hurt when Jack chose to spend most of this leave with the Moores in Bristol rather than with him. Maureen could remember hearing Paddy and Jack make a solemn promise to one another during this leave: if only one of them survived the war, the survivor would look after Paddy's mother and Jack's father.

In October Jack was placed in the Somerset Light Infantry, and in November his regiment crossed the Channel to France. He arrived at the front-line trenches on his nineteenth birthday, 29 November 1917. Not counting a lengthy illness in February 1918, he was involved in military action at various times between November and April, when he was wounded by an English shell exploding behind him. His wounds were serious enough for him to be transferred to a London hospital in May.

In fact, he had made it through the war. He convalesced until October when he was well enough to be moved to an army camp at Ludgershall, Hampshire, where he remained until the war ended on 11 November. He was demobilised in December and arrived home in Belfast two days after Christmas. Both the Lewis brothers had survived the war, and the family was reunited.

But it was not the same for many other families across the United Kingdom. Among them, Mrs Moore and Maureen were mourning the loss of Paddy, killed in action in March.

The relationship between Jack and Mrs Moore is a difficult subject. Even during his convalescence this relationship took on unusual features,

features which would become disturbing to his father and brother. As Jack himself preserved an almost unbroken silence on the subject throughout his life, the evidence is scanty. It would seem that his feelings for her amounted to infatuation for a period of time, but that is about as far as we can go with any certainty. He was not, of course, a Christian at this stage. What we can say is that he kept his promise to Paddy. Mrs Moore now moved to Oxford, and from 1921, when Jack moved out of his college rooms, to 1950, when Mrs Moore was moved to a nursing home, they shared a house. Jack then visited her every day until she died the following year. He came to refer to her as his 'mother'. In making use of his help and support she could be very selfish, and was to become a demanding old lady. Through the years his commitment was steadfast, and he hardly ever complained.

Lewis's first book was a collection of poems called *Spirits in Bondage*. This was published in 1919 when he was only twenty. He had been writing poetry for a number of years, and at this time his ultimate ambition was to be a successful poet. The ideas expressed in these poems were far from Christian, a fact which did not escape his father's notice. Lewis had had a churchgoing childhood, something that was far more common at that time than it is now. It is difficult to say what Christianity meant to either Albert or Flora. Interestingly, however, both of their fathers, Richard Lewis and Thomas Hamilton, were regarded as evangelicals. Perhaps their prayers for their young grandson led to things they never dreamed of. But at this stage the grandson had been a secret atheist since the age of about fourteen.

Meanwhile, Lewis's university career was beginning in earnest. Outstandingly able, he took a double first in a course of studies which included Greek and Latin literature, ancient history, and philosophy. By this time he was definitely aiming at an academic career, and, encouraged by his tutors, went on to study English Literature as well. His father generously continued to give financial support. Lewis's informal reading had already given him a good grounding in English, and he took the exams after a single year—again achieving a first.

In spite of his qualifications, however, it was to be another two years before Lewis gained his desire. During these two years he remained in Oxford, and his father continued his support, although Lewis was not depending only on him. He took various jobs, and in the second of these two years he had a temporary lecturing post at University College. At last, in May 1925, he was chosen as tutor in English at Magdalen College.[1]

Work and faith

Lewis now entered the middle period of his life, which was the longest and, in a sense, most stable period. He kept the same job until 1954. In 1930 he, his brother, Mrs Moore and Maureen moved into their own home, The Kilns, which was to be Lewis's home for the rest of his life. He settled down to his work, made friends and wrote academic books. He also published more poetry, a narrative poem called *Dymer* which came out in 1926.

Nevertheless, there were changes. His father died in 1929, and Mrs Moore in 1951. Maureen married in 1940. But most importantly of all, he became a Christian in 1931.

In certain respects, Lewis's conversion was a very intellectual process. Before becoming a Christian, he believed in a number of alternative ideas, but gradually came to see that none of them fitted the way things really are. At the same time, there was more to his conversion than merely a change of ideas. In chapter 2 we will look at the part played by his growing awareness of his own sin, and of the needs he had as a result of it. In the end, he found that only Christ could meet his need. He himself later wrote an account of his early life and conversion called *Surprised by Joy* (1955). In the meantime, he wrote an allegory about one route to Christian faith, *The Pilgrim's Regress* (1933), which is partly autobiographical.

The Pilgrim's Regress led indirectly to another book, because a publisher who liked it asked Lewis to write a book on suffering. The result was *The Problem of Pain* (1940). This in turn led to something else; it was admired by the BBC's Director of Religious Broadcasting, who invited Lewis to give some radio talks. Lewis agreed that ordinary British people needed to hear what Christianity really is in language they could understand. His aim was evangelistic, and he gave three series of talks in all. Each series was published: *Broadcast Talks* (1942), *Christian Behaviour* (1943), and *Beyond Personality* (1944). These three small books were later put together and revised by Lewis to form one of his most famous books, *Mere Christianity* (1952).

During the Second World War Lewis also worked extremely hard speaking to members of the armed forces. Early in 1941 the Chaplain-in-Chief of the RAF asked if he would become available to speak at air force bases, and from April onwards he travelled all over the country as more and more chaplains made use of him. In term-time he would speak at weekends, in vacations more often, denying himself the holiday he needed. Again, these talks were usually if not always evangelistic.

In such ways Lewis became known to a wider public as he sought to serve God with his gifts. There were other books too: *The Screwtape Letters* (1942), *The Abolition of Man* (1943) and *Miracles* (1947), not to mention his remarkable science fiction trilogy with a Christian background, *Out of the Silent Planet* (1938), *Perelandra* (1943) and *That Hideous Strength* (1945).

It may well be as an author of fairy tales that Lewis is best known. (He would have thought this very strange!) The seven Narnia stories were published annually from 1950 to 1956, and are well loved to this day. Lewis had always loved myths and fairy tales, and now found himself writing his own. 'The whole Narnian story is about Christ,' he explained. 'That is to say, I asked myself, "Supposing that there really was a world like Narnia and supposing it had (like our world) gone wrong and supposing Christ wanted to go into that world and save it (as He did ours). What might have happened." The stories are my answers' (Letter, 5 March 1961).[2] Narnia is a land of talking animals, and Christ appears there as Aslan, the great Lion. So it is not as if Lewis is presenting Aslan as an *alternative* to Christ. Rather, in writing about Aslan he is simply writing about Christ. Of course, he is describing things which Christ has never actually done, never actually said. But if we want to answer the question 'What did Lewis think of Christ?' (a question we will look at in Chapter 3), one of the best ways of finding out is to read the Narnia books.

'Here we have no continuing city'

In what turned out to be Lewis's closing years, there were again a number of changes. In 1954 he changed his university, becoming Professor of Medieval and Renaissance Literature at Cambridge. However, he continued to live in Oxford at the weekends, and so kept up friendships in both places.

Another enormous change was his marriage to a very ill woman. Joy Davidman was an American who had been corresponding with Lewis for some years. After the breakdown of her first marriage, Joy settled in England with her two sons in 1953. But in 1955, with her sons at school in England, the Home Office refused to renew her permission to remain in the country. To enable her to stay, Lewis married her at a registry office the following year, which gave her British citizenship. As far as he was concerned this was not a real marriage, simply the only way of helping Joy out of a legal difficulty, and they remained in their separate homes. However, in October 1956 Joy was found to have advanced cancer and went into hospital. It was thought that the end could not be far off. Lewis pitied her, and by this stage wanted her to be able to come home to The Kilns as his wife to die there. He believed this would be wrong without a marriage performed by a clergyman, and eventually found one willing to carry out the ceremony, which took place in the hospital on 21 March 1957. He believed their marriage was legitimate because Joy's first husband, Bill Gresham, had been married before, so Lewis did not regard Bill's marriage to Joy as a true marriage.

Lewis was now beginning to love Joy. She, in fact, had had intentions towards him for some time, but without her illness it is very doubtful that she would ever have achieved them. Remarkably, the cancer then seems to have gone into retreat for a time, before she finally succumbed to it. In the end, they had a brief but intensely happy marriage until Joy's death in July 1960. As Lewis grieved, he wrote a moving account of his thoughts and experiences, *A Grief Observed* (1961).

Soon, Lewis's own physical condition was far from satisfactory. In June 1961 a doctor found that his prostate gland, kidneys, blood and heart all had things wrong with them. An operation was judged to be too dangerous. Instead, he had to wear a catheter and go on a low-protein diet. Because of his condition he missed two terms at Cambridge, but was able to return in April 1962. During the winter of 1962–63 he began one of his most profound books, *Letters to Malcolm: Chiefly on Prayer* (1964).

By July 1963 his condition was definitely worsening. On 15 July, while he was in a nursing home for one of his regular blood transfusions, he had a heart attack and went into a coma. Unexpectedly he woke from it the following day.

In February that year, Sir George Cospatrick Duff-Sutherland-Dunbar had died. Mrs Moore's daughter Maureen was amazed to discover that, through her father, she was the heir to his title and estate in Caithness. In July she visited Lewis at the nursing home, not having seen him since this happened. He was still very ill, and on the day she came he had not recognised anyone.

'Jack, it is Maureen,' she said.

'No,' he replied, 'it's Lady Dunbar of Hempriggs.'

'Oh, Jack,' she said, 'how could you remember that?'

'On the contrary,' he replied, 'how could I forget a fairy tale?'

Lewis's condition improved somewhat, but he was not able to return to Cambridge and resigned. He died at his Oxford home, The Kilns, on 22 November 1963, one week short of his sixty-fifth birthday.

Notes

1 Pronounced 'Maud-lin'.
2 Quoted in Roger Lancelyn Green and Walter Hooper, *C. S.Lewis: a Biography* (revised edition, Harper Collins, 2002), p.323.

Part 2

Some glimpses of grace

2 Hating sin

Guilty before God

Part and parcel of becoming a Christian is to be made aware of our condition as guilty sinners without excuse, deserving nothing from God except punishment. When the prodigal son came to himself, he confessed, 'I have sinned' (Luke 15:17–21). In another parable, a tax collector who admitted his sin and asked for mercy was justified by God, while a Pharisee who boasted of his moral achievements was not (Luke 18:9–14). The tax collector knew he deserved God's punishment—why else would he ask for mercy?

In his preaching, Jesus called people to repent—to acknowledge their sin and turn away from it (Mark 1:15). The apostle Peter followed his Master's example (Acts 2:38), and so did the apostle Paul (Acts 20:21). Because 'sin is lawlessness' (1 John 3:4), we need to know God's law in order to know and confess our sins (Romans 3:19–20). As we are faced with the law's demands, we realise that we cannot meet them and that our only hope is God's mercy in Christ. In this way, the law of God guides us to Christ (Galatians 3:24). No Christian is without sin (1 John 1:8), yet every Christian struggles with sin and longs to be rid of it (Matthew 5:6).

C. S. Lewis experienced these things for himself.

Pursued by God's law

One of the best ways to trace the process of Lewis's conversion is to read through his letters from 1930 and 1931. A central part of the process was his growing consciousness of sin and its strength. 'I am really trying to become more charitable,' he writes on 26 January 1930. How often does a non-Christian say that? Four days later we find something more remarkable still:

… I have found out ludicrous and terrible things about my own character. Sitting by, watching the rising thoughts to break their necks as they pop up, one learns to know the sort of thoughts that do come. And, will you believe it, one out of every three is a thought of self-admiration: when everything else fails, having had its neck broken, up comes the thought 'What an admirable fellow I am to have broken their necks!' I catch myself posturing before the mirror, so to speak, all day long. I pretend I am carefully thinking out what to say to the next pupil (for *his* good, of course) and then suddenly realise I am really thinking how frightfully clever I'm going to be and how he will admire me. I pretend I am remembering an evening of good fellowship in a really friendly and charitable spirit—and all the time I'm really remembering how good a fellow I am and how well I talked. And then when you force yourself to stop it, you admire yourself for doing *that*. ... There seems to be no end to it. Depth under depth of self-love and self-admiration.

There is no doubt that this shows unusual insight. We may even have to remind ourselves that Lewis was not a Christian when he wrote this. Clearly, something out of the ordinary was going on in him; and it continued to go on. On 7 June he records what he calls 'an interesting and humiliating experience'. A colleague of his, F. H. Lawson, took Lewis to see his father, just settling into a new house after the death of his wife. Lewis describes Lawson as 'a most terrible bore' and was not looking forward to the occasion. However:

When we had been round the whole place and into the house, & when I saw so many things out of Lawson's rooms in Merton[1] brought out here, and saw the affection between them, and realised how Lawson had busied himself about the whole—and then remembered how abominably I had treated *my* father—and worst of all how I had dared to despise Lawson, I was, as I said, humiliated.

For some years Lewis had a burning ambition to be a successful poet. As we saw in Chapter 1, he managed to publish a volume of poems (*Spirits in Bondage*) in 1919 at the age of twenty, and a long narrative poem (*Dymer*) in 1926. However, these were not very successful. On 18 August 1930 we find him ready to own up, not only to his literary failure, but to his sinful motives:

From the age of sixteen onwards I had one single ambition, from which I never wavered, in the prosecution of which I spent every ounce I could, on wh.[ich] I really &

deliberately staked my whole contentment: and I recognise myself as having unmistakably failed in it. ... The side of me which longs, not to write, for no one can stop us doing that, but to be approved as a writer, is not the side of us that is really worth much. And depend upon it, unless God has abandoned us, he will find means to cauterise that side somehow or other.

As these words show, Lewis now believed in God after many years of atheism; but he was not yet a Christian. There is even a sort of admission here that he needed God to work in him in order to defeat his sin. However, other things he wrote make it clear that he was still trusting in himself to do this. Although he admits that there is a 'side' of him which is 'not ... really worth much', he implies that there is another side which is worth a lot more. He was still trying to make himself good by his own efforts. He struggled on for a long time, striving for real goodness, and not completely giving up the hope that he might make progress. He still had the idea that the moral law plus his own efforts could somehow be enough to make him what he should have been. But this hope, and this struggle, were becoming increasingly desperate. On 18 October 1930 he writes: 'My moral history of late has been deplorable. More and more clearly one sees how much of one's philosophy & religion is mere talk: the boldest hope is that concealed somewhere within it there is some seed however small of the real thing...'.

In other words, he is reduced to a very faint hope that somewhere inside him there is some trace of goodness or worthiness. Yet he still clings to this hope! On 17 January 1931 he begins a letter to his friend, Arthur Greeves:

My dear Arthur,

I am much divided in my mind as to whether I should devote this after tea hour—the first free one of the day—to starting a new book or to writing you a letter. The fact that you are in my debt is strong for the first alternative: on the other hand when I hear from you during the week (as I hope I shall) I shall probably be too busy to reply. Then again I have been in a bad temper to day over trifles: and it is too much to face bedtime with the added knowledge of having neglected you as well—so here goes.

We should not misinterpret the words 'you are in my debt' as if they were evidence of a legalistic spirit. Arthur was his closest friend. All Lewis meant was that it was Arthur's turn to write and so, whether he wrote to Arthur or not, he could reasonably expect to hear from Arthur soon. The crucial words here are in the last sentence. At bedtime Lewis would examine himself, thinking over his sins of that day. Perhaps he would confess them to God as well. He knew that he had already 'been in a bad temper … over trifles', and didn't want to have his conscience accuse him of neglecting Arthur on top of that. He felt it would be 'too much to face bedtime with the added knowledge of having neglected you as well'.

We need to be very clear about the attitude that this shows. Why did he want to keep the sins of the day to a minimum? Surely because a shorter list of sins seemed more bearable than a longer one. If it was 'too much' to face bedtime without having written to Arthur, bedtime would not seem quite so daunting once he *had* written. He would have a shorter list of sins to go over. Although he would still feel far from comfortable about himself, he thought that he would not feel as wretched as he might have done otherwise. In other words, he was still trying to satisfy his conscience with his own moral efforts.

In reality, only the death of Christ can ease the guilty conscience. Our conscience is only at peace once we can look at the cross and know that, by trusting in Christ, all our sins were dealt with there once and for all.

At this point Lewis was still trusting in himself, although, as we have seen, this trust was growing weaker. His awareness of sin continued to grow. Yet in spite of the increasing light, it was not until the autumn of 1931 that Lewis finally became a Christian. In a letter to Arthur of 18 October, he describes an important development:

My puzzle was the whole doctrine of Redemption: in what sense the life and death of Christ 'saved' or 'opened salvation to' the world. I could see how miraculous salvation might be necessary: one could see from ordinary experience how sin (e.g. the case of a drunkard) could get a man to such a point that he was bound to reach Hell (i.e. complete degradation and misery) in this life unless something quite beyond mere natural help or effort stepped in. And I could well imagine a whole world being in the same state and similarly in need of miracle.

We needn't worry too much about the words 'Hell ... in this life'. It is true that they do not reflect the Bible's teaching about hell. But that does not mean that Lewis did not also believe in a hell *after* this life; in fact, after his conversion he certainly did, as his later writings show. The important thing here is his awareness of Christian teaching about sin. He knew that Christianity says we all need 'something quite beyond mere natural help or effort' to deal with it. His own efforts to deal with sin had not succeeded, and he was now prepared to believe this, if only he could make sense of 'the whole doctrine of Redemption'. He goes on:

What I couldn't see was how the life and death of Someone Else (whoever he was) 2000 years ago could help us here and now—except in so far as his *example* helped us. And the example business, tho' true and important, is not Christianity: right in the centre of Christianity, in the Gospels and St Paul, you keep on getting something quite different and very mysterious expressed in those phrases I have so often ridiculed ('propitiation'—'sacrifice'—'the blood of the Lamb')...

In these words Lewis is describing nothing less than the dawn of his understanding of the gospel. His understanding was still very hazy at this stage. He describes the teaching he is talking about as 'very mysterious', and later in the letter he says that he still doesn't fully understand how the death of Christ achieved salvation. However, he did not turn back from this point on. His next letter seems to be written on the assumption that he had become a Christian, and the one after that certainly is. By themselves, his letters may not completely prove that he had been converted. But with all the other evidence of God's grace at work in him, some of which we will be looking at in due course, we are on safe ground in dating his conversion to the autumn of 1931. It was the cross that did it. All hope in himself was given up. From now on, he entrusted his sinful self to Christ.

THE SINFULNESS OF SIN

We have looked at some of the insights which Lewis had already gained into sin and its horrors. Throughout his life he continued to hate it and struggle with it. He also continued, from time to time, to produce some very perceptive descriptions of it. We can only look at a few of them here.

...the essential vice, the utmost evil, is Pride. Unchastity, anger, greed, drunkenness, and all that, are mere fleabites in comparison: it was through Pride that the devil became the devil: Pride leads to every other vice: it is the complete anti-God state of mind.

Does this seem to you exaggerated? If so, think it over. I pointed out a moment ago that the more pride one had, the more one disliked pride in others. In fact, if you want to find out how proud you are the easiest way is to ask yourself, 'How much do I dislike it when other people snub me, or refuse to take any notice of me, or shove their oar in, or patronise me, or show off?' The point is that each person's pride is in competition with every one else's pride. ...Pride is competitive by its very nature: that is why it goes on and on. If I am a proud man, then, as long as there is one man in the whole world more powerful, or richer, or cleverer than I, he is my rival and my enemy.

The Christians are right: it is Pride which has been the chief cause of misery in every nation and every family since the world began. Other vices may sometimes bring people together... But pride always means enmity—it *is* enmity. And not only enmity between man and man, but enmity to God.

In God you come up against something which is in every respect immeasurably superior to yourself. Unless you know God as that—and, therefore, know yourself as nothing in comparison—you do not know God at all. As long as you are proud you cannot know God. A proud man is always looking down on things and people: and, of course, as long as you are looking down, you cannot see something that is above you.

Mere Christianity (1952), Book III, Chapter 8

This passage helps us to understand the connection between pride against God and pride against other people. The Pharisee in the parable had both kinds of pride. 'The Pharisee stood up and prayed about himself, "God, I thank you that I am not like other men—extortioners, unjust, adulterers, or even as this tax collector. I fast twice a week; I give tithes of all that I possess"' (Luke 18:11–12). He assumed that God would accept him because of his moral achievements. At the same time, he also assumed that his moral achievements made him better than others.

Lewis wrote a description that fits the Pharisee very well, later in the same chapter. He writes of people who 'pay a pennyworth of imaginary humility to Him [God] and get out of it a pound's worth of Pride towards their fellow-men'. The Pharisee said that he thanked God. This was his 'pennyworth of imaginary humility'. But he went straight on to parade his own achievements, which was his 'pound's worth of Pride'.

If we are foolish enough to offer our own goodness to God, and rely on it to be accepted by him, then we will also look down on other people. Perhaps we will not look down on everyone, at least not in any obvious way. But there will certainly be some people who we think of as worse than ourselves. For the Pharisee it was 'extortioners, unjust, adulterers'. For us it may be murderers, rapists, terrorists. (It may even be Pharisees.) As sinners, we all have a tendency to think of certain other sinners as being in a separate category of badness from ourselves. Christianity corrects this tendency, and teaches us to recognise what Paul recognised: 'in me (that is, in my flesh) nothing good dwells' (Romans 7:18). The words 'in my flesh' mean 'the way I am by birth, without taking the grace and power of God into account'. He means that there is nothing morally good in him at all, apart from what God has given him. Paul was once a Pharisee, but God's love included him.

Lewis also wrote perceptively about sin in itself, as well as about particular sins. The following passage comes after he has just been writing about how all of us, Christian and non-Christian alike, depend on God from moment to moment. We cannot even speak unless he keeps our brains working. We cannot do anything at all unless he keeps our hearts beating, and preserves our lives. Then Lewis says:

And indeed the only way in which I can make real to myself what theology teaches us about the heinousness of sin is to remember that every sin is the distortion of an energy breathed into us—an energy which, if not thus distorted, would have blossomed into one of those holy acts whereof 'God did it' and 'I did it' are both true descriptions. We poison the wine as He decants it into us; murder a melody He would play with us as the instrument. We caricature the self-portrait He would paint. Hence all sin, whatever else it is, is sacrilege. *Letters to Malcolm: Chiefly on Prayer* (1964), 13

This shows a deep awareness of the constant presence of God, and the constant activity of God. One reason why sin is so horrible is that it does not simply abuse a *potential* relationship with God, but an actual relationship. Of course, sinners, in sinning, turn their backs on the possibility of knowing God as their Father, Saviour and Friend—they are really saying that they don't want this. That is the potential relationship. Until they turn towards him, God is not their Father, or Saviour, or Friend. But even though he is not any of those things to them, he is still their Creator and Sustainer. Nothing can change that. He made them, and he continues to sustain them from moment to moment, giving them the breath that they breathe and the strength that they use. That is the actual relationship—and sinners abuse that too. They use the life and strength that God gives them in order to rebel against him. That is what Lewis is describing. In Jonah's words, sinners 'Forsake their own Mercy' (Jonah 2:8). Of course, this applies to the sins of Christians just as much.

* * *

Relapse
Out of the wound we pluck
The shrapnel. Thorns we squeeze
Out of the hand. Even poison forth we suck,
And after pain have ease.

But images that grow
Within the soul have life
Like cancer and, often cut, live on below
The deepest of the knife,

Waiting their time to shoot
At some defenceless hour
Their poison, unimpaired, at the heart's root,
And, like a golden shower,

Unanswerably sweet,
Bright with returning guilt,

Chapter 2

Fatally in a moment's time defeat
Our brazen towers long-built;

And all our former pain
And all our surgeon's care
Is lost, and all the unbearable (in vain
Borne once) is still to bear.

(unknown date)

I know all about the despair of overcoming chronic temptations. It is not serious provided self-offended petulance, annoyance at breaking records, impatience etc doesn't get the upper hand. *No amount* of falls will really undo us if we keep on picking ourselves up each time. We shall of course be v. muddy and tattered children by the time we reach home. But the bathrooms are all ready, the towels put out, & the clean clothes are in the airing cupboard. The only fatal thing is to lose one's temper and give it up. It is when we notice the dirt that God is most present to us: it is the v. sign of His presence.

Letter, 20 January 1942

Note

1 Merton College, Oxford University.

3 In Christ

C. S. Lewis was saved by Jesus Christ. How did Lewis now think of him? The Bible tells us many things about the Saviour. In fact, the whole Bible is about him (John 5:39, 46–47; Luke 24:27), although in different ways. The Christian's Saviour is fully God (Isaiah 9:6; John 1:1; Romans 9:5; Titus 2:13; Hebrews 1:8–10)—only God can save (Isaiah 45:15–21). Yet Jesus Christ is also a man, because it is also true that only a man can save us (Hebrews 2:14–18). He shared our humanity so completely that he was even tempted to sin. The only thing he did not have in common with us was that he never gave in to temptation: he was 'in all points tempted as we are, yet without sin' (Hebrews 4:15).

On the cross, although he had no sin of his own, he took away ours: 'The blood of Jesus Christ [God's] Son cleanses us from all sin' (1 John 1:7). Christians share in both the death, and the new resurrection life, of Christ. The apostle Paul writes: 'I have been crucified with Christ; it is no longer I who live, but Christ lives in me; and the life which I now live in the flesh I live by faith in the Son of God, who loved me and gave himself for me' (Galatians 2:20). And: 'I want to know Christ and the power of his resurrection and the fellowship of sharing in his sufferings, becoming like him in his death, and so, somehow, to attain to the resurrection from the dead' (Philippians 3:10–11, NIV). The connection between Christ and the Christian could not be closer. We were crucified with him when we were converted, our sin being killed and cancelled out; we continue to share in his sufferings here and now; we experience the power of his resurrection here and now; and finally, we will be part of the ultimate 'resurrection from the dead' when he returns. Just as he rose, so shall we: 'Christ the first-fruits, afterwards those who are Christ's at his coming' (1 Corinthians 15:23). Clearly, a Christian's whole existence is bound up with the person of Jesus Christ.

Not only has he died for us, and brought us into acceptance with God, but he also continues to walk with us and strengthen our holiness. Our task is to become like him (1 Corinthians 11:1; Philippians 2:5), which happens as we gaze at his glory (2 Corinthians 3:18). One day this process will be complete: 'when he is revealed, we shall be like him, for we shall see him as he is' (1 John 3:2).

There is no such thing as the Christian life without Christ, the God-man, living in the Christian, and C. S. Lewis knew that.

Who is he?

In common with true Christians everywhere, Lewis believed that Jesus Christ is both God and man. He issued a strong challenge to those who do not believe that Jesus is God. The challenge, quite simply, is to come up with a better explanation. What explanation of Jesus can best account for his recorded words and actions? If he is not God, what is he? Lewis writes:

Among these Jews there suddenly turns up a man who goes about talking as if He was God. He claims to forgive sins. He says He has always existed. He says He is coming to judge the world at the end of time. ...One part of the claim tends to slip past us unnoticed because we have heard it so often that we no longer see what it amounts to. I mean the claim to forgive sins: any sins. ...We can all understand how a man forgives offences against himself. You tread on my toe and I forgive you, you steal my money and I forgive you. But what should we make of a man, himself unrobbed and untrodden on, who announced that he forgave you for treading on other men's toes and stealing other men's money? ...Yet this is what Jesus did. He told people that their sins were forgiven, and never waited to consult all the other people whom their sins had undoubtedly injured. He unhesitatingly behaved as if He was the party chiefly concerned, the person chiefly offended in all offences. This makes sense only if He really was the God whose laws are broken and whose love is wounded in every sin. ...I am trying here to prevent anyone saying the really foolish thing that people often say about Him: 'I'm ready to accept Jesus as a great moral teacher, but I don't accept His claim to be God.' That is the one thing we must not say. A man who was merely a man and said the sort of things Jesus said would not be a great moral teacher. He would either be a lunatic—on a level with the man who says he is a poached egg—or else he would be the Devil of Hell. You must make your choice. Either this man was, and is, the Son of God: or else a madman or something worse. You can shut Him up for a fool, you can spit at Him and kill Him as a demon; or you can fall at His feet and call Him Lord and God. But let us not come with any patronising nonsense about His being a great human teacher. He has not left that open to us. He did not intend to.

Mere Christianity (1952), Book II, Chapter 3

This kind of reasoning has been used by Christians many times since those words were written. For example, it has been widely used in student evangelism. An evangelistic Bible study manual called *Discovering Christianity*, produced by UCCF,[1] sums up this argument as 'Mad, Bad, or God'. Jesus claimed to be God, which sounds like something a madman might say. So was he mad? Even non-Christians will often agree that the moral teachings of Jesus are the very opposite of mad. They are wholesome and good. (Have you ever heard anyone say, 'If we all lived by the Sermon on the Mount the world would be a better place'?) Perhaps, then, Jesus was bad, a wicked man who made his enormous claims not because they were true but in order to deceive people. But that idea doesn't hold up either, because Jesus was executed by the authorities for making those very claims. Even during his trials he continued to make them (Mark 14:61–62; John 18:37). The only reasonable option, therefore, is to believe his claims. Jesus Christ was and is God.

The argument may have been added to a little since Lewis wrote (although Lewis himself elaborated on it in the short piece 'What are we to make of Jesus Christ?' [1950]). However, it is Lewis's foundation that others have built on. As a result, thousands of students and others have been confronted by this strong challenge. Some have been converted.

Lewis also believed, just as firmly, in the humanity of Christ. Although most of the non-Christians we meet are not likely to deny that Jesus was human, this is a truth which the devil has attacked in the past and may do again. The apostle John warned us against those 'who do not confess Jesus Christ as coming in the flesh' (2 John 7). It is just as fatal to deny that Jesus is man as it is to deny that he is God, because, as we saw, only a man can save us (Hebrews 2:14–18).

In the Narnia stories, Lewis invented a world where some animals can think and talk just as well as human beings can. In that world, Christ appears as Aslan, the great Lion. (Lewis was influenced here by the Bible's calling Christ 'the Lion of Judah' in Revelation 5:5.[2]) The third Narnia story, *The Horse and His Boy*, tells how two Talking Horses and two human children escape to the free country of Narnia from a foreign country of oppression and slavery. Near the end of the journey it turns out that Bree, the horse, does not believe that Aslan is a real lion—he thinks that would be beneath Aslan's dignity. He then has to explain why Aslan is called a lion. While he is doing this, 'talking in rather a superior tone with his eyes half shut', Aslan chooses his own way of putting Bree straight. He approaches silently from behind.

'No doubt,' continued Bree, 'when they speak of him as a Lion they only mean he's as strong as a lion or (to our enemies, of course) as fierce as a lion. Or something of that kind. Even a little girl like you, Aravis, must see that it would be quite absurd to suppose he is a *real* lion. Indeed it would be disrespectful. If he was a lion he'd have to be a Beast just like the rest of us. Why!' (and here Bree began to laugh) 'If he was a lion he'd have four paws, and a tail, and W*hiskers*!...Aie, ooh, hoo-hoo! Help!'

For just as he said the word W*hiskers* one of Aslan's had actually tickled his ear. Bree shot away like an arrow to the other side of the enclosure and there turned; the wall was too high for him to jump and he could fly no farther. Aravis and Hwin [the other horse] both started back. There was about a second of intense silence.

Then Hwin, though shaking all over, gave a strange little neigh, and trotted across to the Lion.

'Please,' she said, 'you're so beautiful. You may eat me if you like. I'd sooner be eaten by you than fed by anyone else.'

'Dearest daughter,' said Aslan, planting a lion's kiss on her twitching, velvet nose, 'I knew you would not be long in coming to me. Joy shall be yours.'

Then he lifted his head and spoke in a louder voice.

'Now, Bree,' he said, 'you poor, proud, frightened Horse, draw near. Nearer still, my son. Do not dare not to dare. Touch me. Smell me. Here are my paws, here is my tail, these are my whiskers. I am a true Beast.'

'Aslan,' said Bree in a shaken voice, 'I'm afraid I must be rather a fool.'

'Happy the Horse who knows that while he is still young. Or the Human either. ...'
The Horse and His Boy (1954), Chapter 14

Bree thought it would be 'disrespectful' to suppose that Aslan was 'a Beast just like the rest of us'. But our Saviour truly is a human being just like the rest of us. Of course, in one sense, Bree was right: it was beneath his dignity. But that didn't stop him doing it. Although equality with God has always been his by right, he 'made himself of no reputation, taking the form of a bondservant, and coming in the likeness of men' (Philippians 2:6–7).

Lewis also meditated profoundly on the humanity of Christ in the following poem. The title is taken from Isaiah 53:2; Lewis clearly recognised that this passage refers to Christ.

No Beauty We Could Desire
Yes, you are always everywhere. But I,
Hunting in such immeasurable forests,
Could never bring the noble Hart to bay.

The scent was too perplexing for my hounds;
Nowhere sometimes, then again everywhere.
Other scents, too, seemed to them almost the same.

Therefore I turn my back on the unapproachable
Stars and horizons and all musical sounds,
Poetry itself, and the winding stair of thought.

Leaving the forests where you are pursued in vain
—Often a mere white gleam—I turn instead
To the appointed place where you pursue.

Not in Nature, not even in Man, but in one
Particular Man, with a date, so tall, weighing
So much, talking Aramaic, having learned a trade;

Not in all food, not in all bread and wine
(Not, I mean, as my littleness requires)
But this wine, this bread ... no beauty we could desire.   (unknown date)

This poem is about the fact that mankind can only get into touch with God through Jesus Christ. We cannot find God by looking. We lack the necessary equipment: 'The scent was too perplexing for my hounds'. Why are we not equipped to find God? In part, Lewis seems to be saying that we are simply too small (our 'littleness', last stanza). God is 'always everywhere', so in one sense we are constantly near him, all the time and wherever we go. But that does not amount to a *personal* contact with God. How can we come, as it were, face to face with him—'bring the noble Hart to bay'? Furthermore, our sin prevents us from doing so: 'Other scents, too, seemed to them [my hounds] almost the same'. Nothing and no one can really be a substitute for God, but our minds and hearts are darkened and confused by sin, and in this condition, other things often seem worthy of our deepest devotion. The history of religion proves that when people conduct their own search for objects of worship they will find lots, but not one of them will be the true God. Just as in Athens in Paul's time, among the vast range of false gods, the only 'Unknown God' will be the true one (Acts 17:22–24). 'There is no one who seeks after God' (Romans 3:11).

In the fourth stanza, Lewis concludes that God is 'pursued in vain' when we rely on ourselves. We can only meet him when *he* pursues *us*. And when he pursues us, we meet him in Jesus Christ. That is why he became a man, as the Bible teaches. 'No one has seen God at any time. The only begotten Son, who is in the bosom of the Father, he has declared him' (John 1:18). In Jesus we see 'no beauty we could desire': he was not, frankly, what we were looking for. But it is in him that God is revealed.

The death of deaths

Perhaps surprisingly, there is not a great deal in Lewis's writings about the death of Christ. (But then, how much is there about it in the writings of any other Christian author you like?) But that does not mean that he did not regard it as central. In *Mere Christianity*, having argued that Jesus was and is God, he asks why Jesus came.

Well, to teach, of course; but as soon as you look into the New Testament or any other Christian writing you will find they are constantly talking about something different—

about His death and His coming to life again. It is obvious that Christians think the chief point of the story lies there.

Mere Christianity (1952), Book II, Chapter 4

As we read this chapter in *Mere Christianity*, I think it would be easy to become too disappointed. Lewis may appear to be saying that it does not matter what we believe about Christ's death. He uses the words 'theory' and 'theories' in a dismissive manner; 'Theories about Christ's death are not Christianity,' he writes.

It is indeed vital to distinguish between the biblical belief that Christ's death dealt with human sin, and the 'liberal' belief that it simply shows God's readiness to share our pain. The first is essential to the gospel; the second, when taken on its own, is a false gospel. We may jump to the conclusion that Lewis was not distinguishing between these two. However, if we read more carefully, we shall discover that this conclusion would be unfair. Lewis states very clearly: 'We are told that Christ was killed for us, that His death has washed out our sins, and that by dying He disabled death itself. That is the formula. That is Christianity. That is what has to be believed' (*Mere Christianity* [1952], Book II, Chapter 4).

Lewis is as clear as anyone that Christ's death really and solidly achieved something, and that what it achieved was the defeat of sin and death. When he talks about theories he does not mean theories about what Christ's death achieved; he means theories about *how* it achieved *this*. What he takes care to keep in first place is the fact that it did.

The life of lives

The fact that Christ lives in his people by his Spirit was real to Lewis. Christ conveys his resurrection life to us and makes us holy. '... any conception of Christian fellowship which does not mean primarily fellowship with him is out of court,' Lewis wrote ('Membership', 1945). The New Testament

...talks about Christians 'being born again'; it talks about them 'putting on Christ'; about Christ 'being formed in us'; about our coming to 'have the mind of Christ'.

Chapter 3

Put right out of your head the idea that these are only fancy ways of saying that Christians are to read what Christ said and try to carry it out—as a man may read what Plato or Marx said and try to carry it out. They mean something much more than that. They mean that a real Person, Christ, here and now, in that very room where you are saying your prayers, is doing things to you. ...killing the old natural self in you and replacing it with the kind of self He has.

Mere Christianity (1952), Book IV, Chapter 7

Notice how firmly Lewis puts Christ in control here. Our growth in holiness is not simply a matter of *our* reading the Bible and *our* trying to do what it says; it is a matter of 'Christ ... doing things to you'. The Christian life is a life in which Christ is at work, in resurrection power, rebuilding a human spirit. He has taken over.

* * *

... our imitation of God in this life ... must be an imitation of God incarnate: our model is the Jesus, not only of Calvary, but of the workshop, the roads, the crowds, the clamorous demands and surly oppositions, the lack of all peace and privacy, the interruptions. For this, so strangely unlike anything we can attribute to the Divine life in itself, is apparently not only like, but is, the Divine life operating under human conditions.

The Four Loves (1960), Chapter 1

God did not die for man because of some value he perceived in him. The value of each human soul considered simply in itself, out of relation to God, is zero. As St Paul writes, to have died for valuable men would have been not divine but merely heroic; but God died for sinners. He loved us not because we were lovable, but because he is Love.

'Membership', 1945. See Romans 5:6–8.

Notes

1 Universities and Colleges Christian Fellowship. Lewis's words are also quoted in the more recent *Christianity Explored*.

2 See Walter Hooper and Roger Lancelyn Green, *C. S. Lewis: a Biography* (revised edition, Harper Collins, 2002), pp.323–4.

4 Knowing God

In this chapter we will look at some of the things Lewis said about God's character and about knowing him.

Whose initiative?

If you are a geologist studying rocks, you have to go and find the rocks. They will not come to you, and if you go to them they cannot run away. The initiative lies all on your side. They cannot either help or hinder. But suppose you are a zoologist and want to take photos of wild animals in their native haunts. That is a bit different from studying rocks. The wild animals will not come to you: but they can run away from you. Unless you keep very quiet, they will. There is beginning to be a tiny little trace of initiative on their side.

Now a stage higher; suppose you want to get to know a human person. If he is determined not to let you, you will not get to know him. You have to win his confidence. In this case the initiative is equally divided—it takes two to make a friendship.

When you come to knowing God, the initiative lies on His side. If He does not show Himself, nothing you can do will enable you to find him.

Mere Christianity (1952), Book IV, Chapter 2

This is an important foundation for the subject of knowing God. We need to realise that we are in his hands.

There is a real danger that we will think of God in the same way as a geologist thinks of rocks—as if he were a subject to be studied. We can approach the Bible's teaching about God in a spirit of pride, intending to master the ins and outs of his nature. But if we do that, God will not allow us the great privilege of truly knowing him. God says: 'I dwell in the high and holy place, with him who has a contrite and humble spirit' (Isaiah 57:15).

Knowing God is not much like knowing a subject, like history or car mechanics. It is knowing a person, and a much greater Person than we are.

We cannot approach him on equal terms as you would approach a friend. God lives with those who have a 'humble spirit'. If someone recognises that the God of the Bible is much greater than they are, and comes prepared to worship and submit to him, that person truly knows God.

Lewis reminds us that knowing God involves relying on him. If we are to grasp something of what he is like, he himself needs to show us what he is like. Unless he takes the initiative, our minds can only be defeated in the attempt to think about him: '…no one knows the Son except the Father. Nor does anyone know the Father except the Son, and *he to whom the Son wills to reveal him*' (Matthew 11:27, my italics). Many Christians have discovered that God pursued us before we ever had a thought of turning to him. Jesus' words, 'You did not choose me, but I chose you' (John 15:16) are true of every believer. As Aslan says to Jill in *The Silver Chair* (1953), 'You would not have called to me unless I had been calling to you' (Chapter 2).

The love of God

When we wish to learn of the love and goodness of God by *analogy*—by imagining parallels to them in the realm of human relations—we turn of course to the parables of Christ. But when we try to conceive the reality as it may be in itself, we must beware lest we interpret 'moral attributes' in terms of mere conscientiousness or abstract benevolence. The mistake is easily made because we (correctly) deny that God has passions; and with us a love that is not passionate means a love that is something less. But the reason why God has no passions is that passions imply passivity and intermission. The passion of love is something that happens to us, as 'getting wet' happens to a body: and God is exempt from that 'passion' in the same way that water is exempt from 'getting wet'. He cannot be affected with love, because He *is* love. To imagine that love as something less torrential or less sharp than our own temporary and derivative 'passions' is a most disastrous fantasy.

Miracles (1947), Chapter 11

Here we are dealing with a deep and wonderful subject. Lewis's words are well worth pondering. What is the love of God like? Is it like ours? Yes and no.

As Lewis points out, the parables of Jesus provide us with some illustrations of God's love in human terms. God is like a father who, in spite of being insulted and used by his son, still welcomes him home with open arms when he comes back empty and repenting (Luke 15:11–32). God is like a king who wants anyone and everyone to be guests at his son's wedding (Matthew 22:1–14). God is, not like, but far better than, a magistrate who doesn't care about justice but will give it anyway if he won't get any peace otherwise (Luke 18:1–8).

By reading the parables, Lewis says, we can 'learn of the goodness and love of God by *analogy*'. In these parables, Jesus did not make direct statements about the love of God. Instead, he was trying to help his hearers understand it by describing human situations which bear some resemblance to it. We may feel that these human situations are rather unlikely. Would a king really want ordinary people from the streets (Matthew 22:9) to be honoured guests at his son's wedding? Would a father whose son had treated him so badly be quite so ready to welcome him home with a feast? Yet in a sense that is just the point. God's love is unlikely, amazing. If it is like human love, it is like the most outstanding human love you can possibly imagine. Turning to the book of Hosea, we can say that God is like a husband who keeps on being devoted to a wife who keeps on being unfaithful.

These are analogies of the love of God—pictures of it in terms of astonishing, yet imaginable, human love. But is that what God's love is like in itself? Is it not, in reality, far greater than all human love? Is it not true that there is more to it than even these pictures can get across?

Lewis thought so. He wanted to guard against the idea that the love of God is only as good as the best human love. That is why he says, 'we (correctly) deny that God has passions'. Lewis was an Anglican and would have been thinking here of the Church of England's Thirty-nine Articles, in which God is described as 'without body, parts, or passions' (Article I). However, the Westminster Confession of Faith (Presbyterian) and the 1689 Baptist Confession of Faith both contain exactly the same words (Chapter 2, paragraph 1 in both). What does this mean?

Lewis was a university teacher of English, and so was very well aware that words can change their meaning over time. What he says here accurately reflects the meaning of the word 'passions' when the Articles and Confessions were written, in the sixteenth and seventeenth centuries.

He says that 'passions imply passivity ... The passion of love is something that happens to us'. When we love someone, it is usually because, at least in part, something has *made* us love them. We have been prompted, stirred up, to love them by some factor outside of ourselves. This factor may be one of a number of things. It may be the attractiveness or good qualities of the other person. It may be that the other person is in our family, or has some other close link to us. But the love of God is not like this. He is not prompted or stirred up to love us by our personal qualities. God is not *made* to love people by some factor outside of himself; he is not led into it. The only thing that makes him love is the fact that he *is* love. This is what Lewis means by saying that God's love is not a passion. It is not something that happens to him; it is what he is and does of himself.

Furthermore, as Lewis also says, 'passions imply ... intermission'. Our feelings are sometimes stirred up but they also, inevitably, sometimes fade. The love of God does not. 'I have loved you with an everlasting love' (Jeremiah 31:3).

In making these remarks Lewis wants to guard against two dangers. The first, as we have already seen, is the danger of thinking about God's love only in terms of the best human love. But he also sees that, having corrected that mistake, we may fall into another mistake in the opposite direction. God has no passions; and as Lewis says, 'with us a love that is not passionate means a love that is something less'. We may then start thinking of God's love 'in terms of mere conscientiousness or abstract benevolence'. In other words, we may think that God is like a person who does good simply out of a sense of duty ('mere conscientiousness'); or we may think of his blessings simply as what he happens to do ('abstract benevolence'). When we fall into this trap, some of the joy of being loved by God leaks away. We may have recognised that God's love should not only be thought of as being like the best human love. Yet without realising it, we may then come to see it as something *less* than this. The reality is that the whole force of the irresistible will of God is poured out into loving us and saving us. God's love is not less than passionate—it is more. No one produces it in him; it comes simply from himself, from his very nature, and it goes on and on without a pause. 'God is love' (1 John 4:16).

Graven images

I need Christ, not something that resembles Him. …Images, I must suppose, have their use or they would not have been so popular. (It makes little difference whether they are pictures and statues outside the mind or imaginative constructions within it.) To me, however, their danger is more obvious. Images of the Holy easily become holy images—sacrosanct. My idea of God is not a divine idea. It has to be shattered time after time. He shatters it Himself. He is the great iconoclast [image-smasher]. Could we not almost say that this shattering is one of the marks of His presence? The Incarnation is the supreme example; it leaves all previous ideas of the Messiah in ruins. And most are 'offended' by the iconoclasm; and blessed are those who are not [see Matthew 11:5–6]. But the same thing happens in our private prayers.

A Grief Observed (1961), Chapter 4

It is to be regretted, I believe, that Lewis did not condemn the use of pictures and statues in worship, either here or anywhere else in his writings. They break the Second Commandment. Lewis seems to have had too much of an eye towards what other professing Christians of various kinds do, and have done, in this respect—a subject we will look at in Chapter 9. Nevertheless, his remarks about what is wrong with such images are accurate.

Notice, first, his warning, 'It makes little difference whether they are pictures and statues outside the mind or imaginative constructions within it'. This is an important point. Many Christians today, reading the Ten Commandments, may not find it easy to see that the Second Commandment has much to say to us. When we go to church we are not asked to bow down in front of a picture or statue of Jesus or of a saint. Neither do we do this at home. We do not wear crucifixes. What more is there to be said?

However, at one stage we probably thought that as long as we had not actually committed murder or adultery there was nothing more to be said. Keeping the Sixth and Seventh Commandments seemed straightforward. Then the teaching of the Sermon on the Mount hit home (Matthew 5:21–30). We came to realise that it was not as simple as that. We discovered that our hearts contained thoughts of the same species as these sins.

It is the same with the Second Commandment. There can be graven images in the heart as well as murder in the heart. As Lewis puts it, 'imaginative constructions … My idea of God is not a divine idea'.

Perhaps it is disappointing that Lewis did not mention the Bible at this point. After all, to the extent that our 'idea of God' is taken from the Bible, it *is* 'a divine idea'. The Bible gives us God's own description of himself. If, in our thinking about God, we think about him in the way the Bible describes him, then our idea of him will be accurate. At the same time, we all tend to insert unbiblical elements into our idea of God.

Lewis gives an excellent example of this: the birth, life and death of Christ himself. This, he says, 'leaves all previous ideas of the Messiah in ruins'. Many, if not most, of the Jews were expecting the Messiah to save Israel from the Romans. Accordingly, they imagined him as a military and political figure. Yet he was neither. They, at one point, 'were about to come and take him by force to make him king' (John 6:15); *he* said, 'My kingdom is not of this world' (John 18:36). The popular current ideas of God and his salvation were not accurate. Unbiblical elements had crept in.

The source of the problem was an unbalanced reading of the Bible. The Old Testament spoke of the Messiah bringing glorious victory. But it also spoke of his suffering terrible things, and being 'despised and rejected by men' (Isaiah 53:3). People had emphasised the first and ignored the second. The result was that even the first was misunderstood.

Starting from Genesis 3:15, the victory that God promised was victory over the Enemy who had engineered the Fall. In that chapter God cursed mankind; but he promised Abraham that through his family, 'all the families of the earth shall be blessed' (Genesis 12:3). The curse would be overturned. The effects of the Fall itself would be reversed. That was the victory God had promised—not victory in a military or political tussle in one small country, but victory over sin, death and Satan for all the peoples of the world. Stressing the victory of the Messiah at the expense of his sufferings, people had badly misunderstood the nature of the victory itself.

Lewis's point is that we can all make the same kind of mistake. We all need to have our ideas about God corrected by what the Bible actually says. We, too, are capable of distorting its message by stressing one thing at the expense of another. None of us is free from this danger.[1]

Lewis says 'the same thing happens in our private prayers'. The danger is that we will pray to a god of our own imagining. Some people do only this. If someone is not really converted but thinks he is, then he does not appreciate his true situation before God. He imagines that God is favourable towards him, when in fact God is still angry with him (Psalm 7:11; John 3:18). He thinks that he loves God. But in reality he has 'enmity against God' (Romans 8:7), so the god he loves cannot be the true God. It must, rather, be a product of his own mind.

However, real Christians can commit this sin too. In *Letters to Malcolm* Lewis confesses that he had a tendency to think of God as a 'bright blur'. This, he knew, was an idol which he had to 'break' (Letter 15). Perhaps some of us have had a similar experience. But in other ways, too, we discover again and again that our idea of God was simply not adequate. Often we have prayed for things only to discover, when God granted them to us, that we really expected him not to. The Israelites in the desert 'limited the Holy One of Israel. They did not remember his power' (Psalm 78:41–42). How like us! This is one way in which, as Lewis says, our 'idea of God ... has to be shattered time after time. He shatters it Himself.'

* * *

Don't bother about the idea that God 'has known for millions of years exactly what you are about to pray'. That isn't what it's like. God is hearing you *now*, just as simply as a mother hears a child. The difference His timelessness makes is that this *now* (which slips away from you even as you say the word *now*) is for Him infinite. If you must think of His timelessness at all, don't think of Him *having* looked forward to this moment for millions of years: think that to Him you are always praying this prayer. But there's really no need to bring it in. You have gone into the Temple ('one day in Thy courts is better than a thousand') and found Him, as always, there. That is all you need to bother about.

Letter, 1 August 1949

...you must admit that Scripture doesn't take the slightest pains to guard the doctrine of Divine Impassibility [the teaching that God has no passions]. We are constantly represented as exciting the Divine wrath or pity—even as 'grieving' God. I know this language is analogical. But when we say that, we must not smuggle in the idea that we can throw the analogy away and, as it were, get in behind it to a purely literal truth. All we can really substitute for the analogical expression is some theological abstraction. And the abstraction's value is almost entirely negative. It warns us against drawing absurd consequences from the analogical expression by prosaic extrapolations. By itself, the abstraction 'impassible' can get us nowhere. ...

I suggest two rules for exegetics. (1) Never take the images literally. (2) When the *purport* of the images—what they say to our fear and hope and will and affections—seems to conflict with the theological abstractions, trust the purport of the images every time. For our abstract thinking is itself a tissue of analogies: a continual modelling of spiritual reality in legal or chemical or mechanical terms. Are these likely to be more adequate than the sensuous, organic, and personal images of scripture—light and darkness, river and well, seed and harvest, master and servant, hen and chickens, father and child? The footprints of the Divine are more visible in that rich soil than across rocks or slag-heaps.

Letters to Malcolm: Chiefly on Prayer (1964), 10

Note

1 An excellent article on this subject is Maurice Roberts, 'A Well Balanced Christianity', *The Christian's High Calling* (Edinburgh: Banner of Truth, 2000). The whole book should be very highly prized.

5 Pressing towards the goal

The glorious future of Christians played an important part in Lewis's thinking. In this chapter we will look at some of the things he said about it. We will begin with a poem. Although this poem is more about the journey than the destination, it does speak about the destination too.

Pilgrim's Problem
By now I should be entering on the supreme stage
Of the whole walk, reserved for the late afternoon.
The heat was to be over now; the anxious mountains,
The airless valleys and the sun-baked rocks, behind me.

Now, or soon now, if all is well, come the majestic
Rivers of foamless charity that glide beneath
Forests of contemplation. In the grassy clearings
Humility with liquid eyes and damp, cool nose
Should come, half-tame, to eat bread from my hermit hand.
If storms arose, then in my tower of fortitude—
It ought to have been in sight by this—I would take refuge;
But I expected rather a pale mackerel sky,
Feather-like, perhaps shaking from a lower cloud
Light drops of silver temperance, and clovery earth
Sending up mists of chastity, a country smell,
Till earnest stars blaze out in the established sky
Rigid with justice; the streams audible; my rest secure.

I can see nothing like all this. Was the map wrong?
Maps can be wrong. But the experienced walker knows
That the other explanation is more often true.   (1952)

One reason this poem appeals to me is that I am an (amateurish) walker myself. The 'other explanation' is, indeed, 'more often true'! Lewis enjoyed walking, and here he compares the Christian life to a journey on foot. Every Christian is a 'pilgrim', as the Bible tells us (1 Peter 2:11). This world is not our home; we are 'strangers and pilgrims on the earth' (Hebrews 11:13). We are travelling through this world, and our destination is heaven.

However, if we are ever to reach heaven, something has to happen in us while we are still here. 'Unless your righteousness exceeds the righteousness of the scribes and Pharisees, you will by no means enter the kingdom of heaven' (Matthew 5:20). 'Pursue ... holiness, without which no one will see the Lord' (Hebrews 12:14). All those who go to heaven are holy, and righteous.

A person begins to be holy when he or she is converted. James 2:17 tells us that 'faith by itself, if it does not have works, is dead'. In other words, genuine faith will always have practical consequences for the way we live. Anything which is *called* faith, but which does not produce any works, is not really faith at all.

This is true even in the case of those who are only converted very late in life. The dying thief only had faith for his last few hours. Yet for those few hours, what a changed man he was! Earlier that same day, even as he hung on his own cross, he had hurled abuse at our Saviour (Matthew 27:42–44). He had not believed that a man hanging, like himself, in public disgrace on a cross—to die that very day—could possibly be the Christ. But within a few hours, he was prepared to rebuke his fellow-criminal for continuing to mock Jesus (Luke 23:39–40). In doing so he also rebuked his own former self. Unbelief about who Jesus was, was not for him any longer. Therefore, neither was the mocking which gave that unbelief such scornful expression. Now he knew that Jesus would inherit a kingdom one day. He humbly asked for a place in that kingdom—a place he knew he did not deserve. 'We receive the due reward of our deeds ... Lord, remember me when you come into your kingdom' (Luke 23:41–42). What a strong and gracious promise he was given in answer: 'Assuredly, I say to you, today you will be with me in paradise' (Luke 23:43)! The faith of the dying thief was not dead faith. It changed his last hours of life, and it changed his eternity.

For most of us, the road to paradise is longer. We are to be changed, and to go on being changed, 'from glory to glory, just as by the Spirit of the Lord' (2 Corinthians 3:18). In this poem, Lewis expresses his disappointment that he himself was not further on in this process than he was.

He does this by comparing the stages of the process to the stages of a day's walk. The walk has been well planned. The challenges were all to come earlier in the day. The heat of noon found the pilgrim tackling 'anxious mountains,/ The airless valleys and the sun-baked rocks'. He is looking forward to easier country, where he can walk on the level through a land of rivers and forests. He will be there 'soon now, if all is well'. He can see this more restful stage in his mind's eye, and spends the central and longest section of the poem describing it. But then, as he looks again at the country that actually surrounds him, he has to admit, 'I can see nothing like all this.' Many a walker, looking from the map to the country and back again, has had exactly the same sensations!

Applying this to the spiritual life, Lewis looks forward with longing to what he ought to be. Paul wrote: 'reaching forward to those things which are ahead, I press toward the goal' (Philippians 3:13–14). Lewis was eager to do the same; but, like Paul, he could also say, 'I do not consider that I have made it my own' (Philippians 3:13, ESV).

What, exactly, was Lewis looking forward to? The central section of the poem answers this question. He was looking forward to greater holiness. He anticipates that the later stages of the Christian life will, in one sense, be easier—but notice in what sense. It is not that he imagines less holiness will be required, as if God simply lets us off some things or weakens his demands. Rather, he looks forward to a stage at which the holiness God has required all along will at last come more naturally.

He expresses this by using some striking pieces of imagery to describe various godly qualities. There should be 'majestic/ Rivers of foamless charity ... Forests of contemplation', and much more, in him. The picture of humility as a deer or some timid animal 'with liquid eyes and damp, cool nose' seems especially appropriate. How do we get it to come to us? It is a delicate procedure. Humility, like the animal, is liable to bound away in a split second the moment the wrong kind of consciousness intrudes. As someone said, 'The moment you think you've got it you realise you haven't.'

But one day we will be all that we should be. In heaven, 'his servants shall serve him' (Revelation 22:3). All true Christians are pilgrims travelling to the same destination. Our destination is heaven, and our destination is holiness.

Glory

The Bible promises 'glory' to Christians. One example of this is 2 Corinthians 4:17—'our light affliction, which is but for a moment, is working for us a far more exceeding and eternal weight of glory'. This verse provided Lewis with the title for a sermon he preached in 1941, 'The Weight of Glory'. In this sermon he describes what the promise of glory means. Usually, 'glory' means fame. Lewis concludes that, in part, this is actually what is promised to Christians. 'But not,' he writes, 'fame conferred by our fellow creatures—fame with God, approval or (I might say) "appreciation" by God. … nothing can eliminate from the parable the divine *accolade*,[1] "Well done, thou good and faithful servant".' Lewis continues by explaining that it is right for us to be happy when we succeed in pleasing those we ought to please. The child is happy when the parent praises him or her. In the same way, part of our happiness in heaven will come from the fact that God is happy with us. We should desire this.[2]

I am not forgetting how horribly this most innocent desire is parodied in our human ambitions, or how very quickly, in my own experience, the lawful pleasure of praise from those whom it was my duty to please turns into the deadly poison of self-admiration. But I thought I could detect a moment—a very, very short moment—before this happened, during which the satisfaction of having pleased those whom I rightly loved and rightly feared was pure. And that is enough to raise our thoughts to what may happen when the redeemed soul, beyond all hope and nearly beyond belief, learns at last that she has pleased Him whom she was created to please. There will be no room for vanity then. She will be free from the miserable illusion that it is her doing. With no taint of what we should now call self-approval she will most innocently rejoice in the thing that God has made her to be, and the moment which heals her old inferiority complex for ever will also drown her pride…. Perfect humility dispenses with modesty. If God is satisfied with the work, the work may be satisfied with itself…. I can imagine someone saying that he dislikes my idea of heaven as a place where we are patted on the back. But proud misunderstanding is behind that dislike. In the end that Face which is the delight or the terror of the universe must be turned upon each of us either with one expression or with the other, either conferring glory inexpressible or inflicting shame that can never be cured or disguised. I read in a periodical the other day that the fundamental thing is how we think of God. By God Himself, it is not! How God thinks of us is not only more important, but infinitely more important. Indeed, how we think of Him is of no importance except in so far as it is related to how He thinks of us. It is written that we shall "stand before" Him, shall appear, shall be inspected. The promise of glory is the promise, almost incredible and only possible by the work of Christ, that some of us, that any of us who really chooses, shall actually survive that examination, shall find approval, shall please God. To please God … to be a real ingredient in the divine happiness … to be loved by God, not merely pitied, but delighted in as an artist delights in his work or a father in a son—it seems impossible, a weight or burden of glory which our thoughts can hardly sustain. But so it is.

How do we think of the goal of the Christian life? Do we see it in terms of keeping God's commandments? That is a right and biblical way to see it (John 14:15; 1 Corinthians 7:19). Do we think of it in terms of being God's servants? That, too, is entirely correct (Romans 6:22; 1 Peter 2:16). But we should also see it in terms of pleasing God. Paul told the Colossians that he prayed for them, that they would 'walk worthy of the Lord, fully pleasing him' (Colossians 1:10).

Perhaps this perspective brings out more clearly the loving personal relationship that Christians have with God. Because we love him, we want to please him. In this life, I think, we can only have a dim and partial awareness that we have pleased him. To be sure, the Bible tells us what pleases him, but we are not going to be very reliable judges of how well we have lived up to it. And in any case, we never do live up to it as well as we should. But the time is coming when we shall please him fully, and for ever. We shall then know for certain that God is well pleased with us. He will look at us and be completely satisfied with what he sees.

He will rejoice over you with gladness,
He will quiet you with his love,
He will rejoice over you with singing. (Zephaniah 3:17)

That will be glory!

The same situation, Lewis says, will both heal our inferiority complex and drown our pride. On the one hand, we have a secret longing to be admired by others. That will be gone for ever because we will be content with what God thinks of us. On the other hand, we also have an attitude inside us that says, 'I don't care what others think of me—I *know* I'm special!' That, too, will vanish because we will know perfectly well that we do not deserve the glory God will heap on us (Romans 8:29–30). Lewis calls the idea that we can make ourselves pleasing to God a 'miserable illusion', from which we shall be entirely free. It is glory without merit.

Resurrection!

Lewis believed that, at least in his time, Christians did not think enough about their own resurrection. In *Miracles* he quotes a remark he had heard more than once, 'Heaven is a state of mind'. He comments that a person's state of mind is a state of his or her spirit, and that heaven, although it *is* that, is not *just* that.

Christian teaching by saying that God made the world and called it good teaches that Nature or environment cannot be simply irrelevant to spiritual beatitude [blessedness]... By teaching the resurrection of the body it teaches that Heaven is not merely a state of the spirit but a state of the body as well: and therefore a state of Nature as a whole. ...We are never *merely* in a state of mind. The prayer and the meditation made in howling wind or quiet sunshine, in morning alacrity or evening resignation, in youth or age, good health or ill, may be equally, but are differently, blessed. Already in this present life we have all seen how God can take up all these seeming irrelevancies into the spiritual fact and cause them to bear no small part in making the blessing of that moment to be the particular blessing it was—as fire can burn coal and wood equally but a wood fire is different from a coal one. From this factor of environment Christianity does not teach us to desire a total release. We desire, like St. Paul, not to be un-clothed but to be re-clothed: to find not the formless Everywhere-and-Nowhere but the promised land, that Nature which will be always and perfectly—as present Nature is partially and intermittently—the instrument for that music which will then arise between Christ and us.

... I suspect that our conception of Heaven as *merely* a state of mind is not unconnected with the fact that the specifically Christian virtue of Hope has in our time grown so languid. Where our fathers, peering into the future, saw gleams of gold, we see only the mist, white, featureless, cold and never moving.

The thought at the back of all this negative spirituality is really one forbidden to Christians. They, of all men, must not conceive spiritual joy and worth as things that need to be rescued or tenderly protected from time and place and matter and the senses. Their God is the God of corn and oil and wine. He is the glad Creator. He has become Himself incarnate. ...To shrink back from all that can be called Nature into negative spirituality is as if we ran away from horses instead of learning to ride. There is in our present pilgrim condition plenty of room (more room than most of us like) for abstinence and renunciation and mortifying our natural desires. But behind all asceticism the thought should be, 'Who will trust us with the true wealth if we cannot be trusted even with the wealth that perishes?' Who will trust me with a spiritual body if I cannot control even an earthly body? These small and perishable bodies we now have were given to us as ponies are given to schoolboys. We must learn to manage: not that we may some day be free of horses altogether but that some day we may ride bareback, confident and rejoicing, those greater mounts, those winged, shining and world-shaking horses which perhaps even now expect us with impatience, pawing and snorting in the King's stables. Not that the gallop would be of any value unless it were a gallop with the King; but how else—since He has retained His own charger—should we accompany Him?

Miracles (1947), Chapter 16

Lewis is very clear that the resurrection of our bodies, and the new earth, are central Christian teachings. In 1 Corinthians 15, Paul shows that there is no such thing as Christianity with resurrection left out. Since Christ has risen from the dead, so shall we: 'Christ the first-fruits, afterwards those who are Christ's at his coming' (verse 23).

Lewis writes, 'Heaven is not merely a state of the spirit but a state of the body as well: *and therefore a state of Nature as a whole.*' In other words, there is a connection between the doctrine of the resurrection and the doctrine of the new earth. Resurrected bodies need somewhere to live, and the Bible teaches that God will provide this. 'Now I saw a new heaven and a new earth, for the first heaven and the first earth had passed away. ...Then he who sat on the throne said, "Behold, I make all things new" ' (Revelation 21:1, 5).

Then Lewis adds some fascinating thoughts. Do we not know already, by experience, that physical factors can play a part in our prayers and meditations? These physical factors include the condition of our bodies: 'in morning alacrity or evening resignation, in youth or age, good health or ill'. We may like to think that such things should make no difference to our prayers, but they do. And physical factors around us have a part to play as well. A prayer or meditation made in howling wind may have a very different character from one made in quiet sunshine, Lewis says. This need not mean that one is worse than the other; they are simply different. They 'may be equally, but are differently, blessed'. We have all experienced how God can use these physical factors 'to bear no small part in making the blessing of that moment to be the particular blessing it was'. Lewis was alert to what the creation around him was doing. If we are not, I think we lose a great deal.

But in this fallen world, and with our fallen nature, our surroundings only play this part 'partially and intermittently'. The New Creation, with our resurrected bodies living in it, will be 'always and perfectly ... the instrument for that music which will then arise between Christ and us'.

God created us both spirit and body, and God saves us both spirit and body. In this life God 'gives us richly all things to enjoy' (1 Timothy 6:17). In the next life he will do so far more. In Nature made new there will be nothing we cannot enjoy, nothing in which we cannot taste the goodness of God, and we ourselves will be fully alert to that goodness. Our experience of the new earth will be an uninterrupted torrent of adoration.

At the same time, Lewis reminds us that in this life there is 'plenty of room ... for abstinence and renunciation and mortifying our natural desires'. At present, the relationship between spirit and body is often uneasy. Denying ourselves is at the very heart of the Christian life (Matthew 16:24–26); and this often involves denying our bodily desires. Even Christ denied himself (Romans 15:3). He denied himself in coming to this world at all (Philippians 2:5–7), and his sufferings were the ultimate in self-denial. The servant is not greater than his Master; we too are often called upon to submit to pain.

This is not simply because we will be persecuted. It is also because, in our fallenness, our bodily desires are unruly and need to be disciplined. The apostle Paul knew this: 'Do you not know that those who run in a race all run, but one receives the prize? Run in such a way that you may obtain it. And everyone who competes for the prize is temperate in all things. Now they do it to obtain a perishable crown, but we for an imperishable crown. … I discipline my body and bring it into subjection, lest, when I have preached to others, I myself should become disqualified' (1 Corinthians 9:24–27). Notice that Paul wrote of this as something he was still doing, not something he had fully achieved.

But as we set about subduing our bodies, we are to remember why. It is not so that we will be able to manage without them one day, but rather so that we may have a 'spiritual body'. In using the phrase 'spiritual body', Lewis is referring to 1 Corinthians 15:44. Glorious, imperishable bodies will be ours. But if they are ever to be ours, we must live in this world as Paul did. He was afraid of being 'disqualified' if he did not run hard for the prize. We, too, must work hard at disciplining our bodies now if we are to gain that 'imperishable crown' in the end.

Finally, Lewis adds another very necessary reminder. Not even glorious resurrection bodies would be of any value unless, in them, we will be 'with the King'. With resurrection eyes we will see him. The Lamb is the very light of heaven (Revelation 21:23). With such a prospect before us, we heed his own words, 'Be faithful until death, and I will give you the crown of life' (Revelation 2:10).

* * *

The New Testament has lots to say about self-denial, but not about self-denial as an end in itself. We are told to deny ourselves and to take up our crosses in order that we may follow Christ; and nearly every description of what we shall ultimately find if we do so contains an appeal to desire. … Indeed, if we consider the unblushing promises of reward and the staggering nature of the rewards promised in the Gospels, it would seem that Our Lord finds our desires, not too strong, but too weak. We are half-hearted creatures, fooling about with drink and sex and ambition when infinite joy is offered us, like an ignorant child who wants to go on making mud pies in a slum because he cannot imagine what is meant by the offer of a holiday at the sea. We are far too easily pleased.

'The Weight of Glory', 1941

Chapter 5

Evensong
Now that night is creeping
O'er our travailed senses,
To Thy care unsleeping
We commit our sleep.
Nature for a season
Conquers our defences,
But th'eternal Reason
Watch and ward will keep.

All the soul we render
Back to Thee completely,
Trusting Thou wilt tend her
Through the deathlike hours,
And all night remake her
To Thy likeness sweetly,
Then with dawn awake her
And give back her powers.

Slumber's less uncertain
Brother soon will bind us
—Darker falls the curtain,
Stifling-close 'tis drawn:
But amidst that prison
Still Thy voice can find us,
And, as Thou has risen,
Raise us in Thy dawn.
(unknown date)

Notes

1 It is Lewis who puts this word in italics. This is not because he wants to lay special stress on it, but because it is a French word which he regarded as not fully absorbed into the English language.

2 In the following quotation, rows of four dots show where I have missed something out, and rows of three dots are Lewis's own.

Part 3

Some areas of concern

6 The Bible

'I cannot claim to have a clearly worked out position about the Bible or the nature of Inspiration', wrote C. S. Lewis. 'That is a subject on which I w[oul]d. gladly learn: I have nothing to teach.' These significant words come in a private letter dated 4 February 1949. Lewis was consistent with this in his public writings too. He seldom wrote about the nature of the Bible directly, and almost never for very long; and when he did express his ideas on the subject, he often added that he was not sure about them.

We may well regret that Lewis was never given the sound teaching on the nature of the Bible which he said he would have been glad to receive. As a result, his ideas about it were mistaken in a number of different ways, as we shall see.

History

We know that what we call revelation took place over a period of time. God has revealed himself, and his plan of salvation, to the human race. But he did not do so all at once; it was a process. Abraham did not know as much about Christ as Peter knew. 'Your father Abraham rejoiced to see my day,' said Jesus to the Jews, 'and he saw it and was glad' (John 8:56). Abraham knew enough about Christ to trust him for salvation, but this does not mean he knew the whole contents of the four Gospels before they were written. Gradually, over time, God revealed more and more. Finally, in the New Testament, his plan of salvation was fully disclosed. The Old Testament pointed forward; it contained 'a shadow of the good things to come' (Hebrews 10:1). The gospel is in the Old Testament, but in a shadowy form. It was not yet time for the full glory of the gospel to be made known. No one but Christ should have the honour of revealing all the riches of salvation to the world. 'God, who at various times and in different ways spoke in time past to the fathers by the prophets, has in these last days spoken to us by his Son, whom he has appointed heir of all things' (Hebrews 1:1–2). A great Christian leader of the fourth and fifth centuries, Augustine of Hippo, summed it up like this: 'For what is the Old Testament but a concealed form of the New? And what is the New Testament but the revelation of the Old?'[1]

Lewis would have agreed with most or all of the last paragraph. But he also added other ideas of his own. Let us now try to grasp what these other ideas were.

In 1944, when Lewis had become known as a speaker on Christianity, he was invited to Hayes in Middlesex to speak to workers at the Electrical and Musical Industries (EMI) factory. The format agreed was that they would pose questions which he would then try to answer. (It was much like a one-man version of a 'Grill-a-Christian' event, which Christian Unions sometimes hold today.) The Electrical and Musical Industries Christian Fellowship, which had invited him, then published the questions and answers as a pamphlet called *Answers to Questions on Christianity*. Here is one of the questions together with the answer Lewis gave. The word 'fabulous' here means something that is a *fable*—something that is not literally true.

Question 10

The Bible was written thousands of years ago for people in a lower state of mental development than today. Many portions seem preposterous in the light of modern knowledge. In view of this, should not the Bible be rewritten with the object of discarding the fabulous and reinterpreting the remainder?

Lewis: First of all as to the people in a lower state of mental development. I am not so sure what lurks behind that. If it means that people ten thousand years ago did not know a good many things that we know now, of course, I agree. But if it means that there has been any advance in *intelligence* in that time, I believe there is no evidence for any such thing. The Bible can be divided into two parts—the Old and the New Testaments. The Old Testament contains fabulous elements. The New Testament consists mostly of teaching, not of narrative at all: but where it *is* narrative, it is, in my opinion, historical. As to the fabulous element in the Old Testament, I very much doubt if you would be wise to chuck it out. What you get is something *coming gradually into focus*. First you get, scattered through the heathen religions all over the world—but still quite vague and mythical—the idea of a god who is killed and broken and then comes to life again. No one knows where he is supposed to have lived and died; he's not historical. Then you get the Old Testament. Religious ideas get a bit more focused. Everything is now connected with a particular nation. And it comes still more into focus as it goes on. Jonah and the Whale (the Book of Jonah), Noah and his Ark (Genesis 6–8) are fabulous; but the court history of King David (2 Samuel 2—1 Kings 2) is probably as reliable as the court history of Louis XIV. Then, in the New Testament the *thing really happens*. The dying god really appears—as a historical Person, living in a definite place and time. If we *could* sort out all the fabulous elements in the earlier stages and separate them from the historical ones, I think we might lose an essential part of the whole process. That is my own idea.

Notice Lewis's phrase, 'coming gradually into focus'. If we took that phrase on its own, it would in fact be a very good description of the way that God has revealed himself and his gospel over a period of time, with more and more details becoming clear. And this is what Lewis means, but he adds two other ideas of his own:

(1) He regards the process as having *three* main stages, not two. The Old and New Testaments are the second and third stages, according to him. The first stage is, in his words, 'the idea of a god who is killed and broken and then comes to life again' which is 'scattered through the heathen religions all over the world'.

(2) He assumes that earlier parts of the process, including parts of the Old Testament, are not literally true.

Both of these added ideas are very serious errors. We will leave the first one to be considered in Chapter 8, but we must now look at the second. It is unlike Lewis to make an assumption with no adequate basis, but that is exactly what he does here. We can agree with him when he says that the gospel comes 'gradually into focus' as God's revelation unfolds. But according to him, this must involve some accounts given in the Old Testament not being historically true. And this is a pure assumption; he has no reason at all to think this. Why should it not be possible for history that is completely true in itself to present the gospel in a form that is only shadowy?

We can guess at what caused him to fall into this error. He lived at a time when very few people, even among professing Christians, were prepared to stand up for the historical truth of the Old Testament. It was widely accepted that accounts such as those of Noah and Jonah were never meant to be taken literally. Furthermore, when we remember Lewis's idea that certain stories in ancient pagan religions were part of the same process as the Old Testament, it is easy to see that this would have influenced him away from recognising the Old Testament as historical. He knew that the pagan stories were not historical, yet he believed that they contained a glimpse of the truth; he knew the Old Testament contained the truth, yet saw no problem with regarding it as partly unhistorical.

Of course, there are parts of the Bible which are not meant to be taken as history. Jesus's parables are a clear example of this. The Old Testament contains similar passages—see, for example, 2 Samuel 12:1–7, and Isaiah 5:1–7. But it is obvious in both of these passages that the story is not meant to be taken as literally true. Every Bible account which is *meant* to be read as history, is history.

In fact, Lewis would have agreed with that. However, he also thought that some accounts, such as those of the Creation, Noah, Job and Jonah, were never meant to be taken as historically true. For example, elsewhere he refers to the books of Jonah and Job like this: '*Jonah*, a tale with as few even pretended historical attachments as *Job*, grotesque in incident and surely not without a distinct, though of course edifying, vein of typically Jewish humour' ('Fern-seed and Elephants', 1959). If we disagree with Lewis over this, we need to be clear about exactly where the disagreement lies. Lewis is *not* saying, 'I know that Jonah and Job were written as history, but I refuse to accept them as history.' Rather, he is saying, 'I don't believe that Jonah and Job were written as history, so I don't regard them as history.' (However, Jonah is also mentioned in 2 Kings 14:25 and by Jesus, e.g. Matthew 12:39–41. Job is also mentioned in Ezekiel 14:14, 20 and James 5:11.)

We must also admit that, even when Lewis accepted a part of the Bible as history, he did not regard it as perfect history. In the extract quoted earlier he says that the account of King David is 'probably as reliable as the court history of Louis XIV' (a French king). This falls short of saying that it contains no mistakes.

He had the same attitude to New Testament history. He described John's Gospel as 'reportage—though it may no doubt contain errors—pretty close up to the facts' ('Fern-seed and Elephants', 1959). In practice, he accepted the Gospels entirely, including the miracles. He often referred to the Gospels and quoted them, as Appendix 3 shows, and there is no record that he ever regarded any particular passage as being in error. But it is dangerous and wrong to admit the possibility of errors in the Bible. If it did contain mistakes, how could we tell the difference between what was correct and what was not?

This leads on to another subject.

What does it mean for the Bible to be God's Word?

The words of the LORD are pure words,
Like silver tried in a furnace of earth,
Purified seven times. (Psalm 12:6)

In Scripture the number seven often points to perfection or completeness. Here, it is being used to say that God's Word is perfect, so thoroughly pure that no flaw whatsoever can be found in it. It contains no mistakes. All that it says is true, without qualification.

So where do we find God's Word? How can we get at it? The Bible's answer is that the Bible itself is God's Word. We can see this from a number of passages. 'All Scripture is breathed out by God,' writes Paul to Timothy (2 Timothy 3:16, ESV). Paul leaves no exceptions here; he does not allow for any parts of the Bible which are not quite God's Word. All Scripture comes from God's mouth and must therefore be completely pure.

Of course, it is not as if the Bible dropped from heaven ready-made. The Bible does not hide the fact that it was written by human authors. These human authors leave their marks on the finished product, too. As we read, we can tell the difference between Isaiah's writing and Amos's writing, or between Paul's style and John's. The Bible was written by people, but they were people in whom God was at work in a unique way, so as to ensure that what they wrote was exactly what he wanted. Peter describes it like this: 'men spoke from God as they were carried along by the Holy Spirit' (2 Peter 1:21, NIV).

As we have seen, Lewis did not regard the Bible as error-free. This is because he did not think that the Bible simply *is* the Word of God. By far the longest statement of his views on the subject comes in his book *Reflections on the Psalms*, written fairly late in his life. Here is an extract:

... something originally merely natural ... will have been raised by God above itself, qualified by Him and compelled by Him to serve purposes which of itself it would not have served. ...I take it that the whole Old Testament consists of the same sort of material as any other literature—chronicle (some of it obviously pretty accurate), poems, moral and political diatribes, romances, and what not; but all taken into the service of God's word. Not all, I suppose, in the same way. There are prophets who write with the clearest awareness that Divine compulsion is upon them. There are chroniclers whose intention may have been merely to record. There are poets like those in the *Song of Songs* who probably never dreamed of any but a secular and natural purpose in what they composed. ...On all of these I suppose a Divine pressure; of which not by any means all need have been conscious.

The human qualities of the raw materials show through. Naïvety, error, contradiction, even (as in the cursing Psalms) wickedness are not removed. The total result is not 'the Word of God' in the sense that every passage, in itself, gives impeccable science or history. It carries the Word of God; and we (under grace, with attention to tradition and to interpreters wiser than ourselves, and with the use of such intelligence and learning as we may have) receive that word from it not by using it as an encyclopædia or an encyclical but by steeping ourselves in its tone or temper and so learning its over-all message.

Reflections on the Psalms (1958), Chapter 11

When Lewis says that the Bible (in this case, the Old Testament) 'carries the Word of God', that gives his view in a nutshell. Elsewhere in the same chapter he describes it as the 'vehicle' of the Word of God. He seems to be regarding it as the means by which God's Word reaches us, but not as being itself, in all its parts, that Word.

Later in the chapter he compares Scripture with the person of Christ. This is a good comparison. Although he is truly human as well as being truly God, Christ is perfect. Strangely, however, this did not lead Lewis to acknowledge that it is the same with the Bible. Although it is a human book as well as God's book, it is perfect.

Lewis's view, though mistaken, is not so completely different from the truth that it prevented him from benefitting from Scripture at all. He still talks about 'steeping ourselves in its tone or temper and so learning its over-all message', which is obviously a good thing to do. Yet his belief that it contains errors perhaps hampered him from taking it, in all its details, with quite the seriousness it deserves.

The two aspects of Lewis's thinking about the Bible which we have looked at so far are both important, but now we come to an aspect which is perhaps the most important of all.

Christ in Scripture

Jesus Christ is the main theme of all Scripture, Old Testament as well as New. He himself said, 'the Scriptures … testify of me'; and he very plainly added, 'Moses … wrote about me' (John 5:39, 46). Speaking to the two disciples on the road to Emmaus, 'beginning at Moses and all the prophets, he expounded to them in all the Scriptures the things concerning himself' (Luke 24:27). 'All the Scriptures' are about Christ. The New Testament contains hundreds of quotations from the Old Testament, which shows how closely the two fit together. The New Testament writers saw Christ all over the Old Testament.

What was Lewis's view? He recognised this in part. But he was also hampered by his idea that the Bible *began* as ordinary human literature which was *then* taken up by God and somehow made into the vehicle of his Word. This is what lies behind the following statement ('He' refers to Christ here): 'He accepted—indeed he claimed to be—the second meaning of Scripture' (*Reflections on the Psalms*, Chapter 11). Lewis does recognise here that Christ can be found in the Old Testament. However, he thinks that Christ is only 'the second meaning'. In reality, our Lord Jesus Christ is not the second meaning of Scripture, but the first!

Lewis says this because he thinks the Old Testament writers, or at least many of them, were writing about other things. God then took their work and moulded it, perhaps through a series of versions, to say something about his Son. They themselves, however, were not consciously writing about Christ at all. This would mean that Jesus is the second meaning of the Old Testament, but not the first, not the meaning the authors intended.

What sort of first meaning did Lewis have in mind? Let's look at an example. Commenting on Psalm 45, he refers to the fact that the Anglican Book of Common Prayer lays down this psalm for use on Christmas Day.[2] (It might be a good idea to read the psalm before reading Lewis's comments.)

… Psalm 45 … shows us so many aspects of the Nativity we could never get from the carols or even (easily) from the gospels. This in its original intention was obviously a laureate ode on a royal wedding. … And simply as a marriage ode … it is magnificent. But it is far more valuable for the light it throws on the Incarnation …

…the Psalm restores Christmas to its proper complexity. The birth of Christ is the arrival of the great warrior and the great king. Also of the Lover, the Bridegroom, whose beauty surpasses that of man [a reference to verse 2]. But not only the Bridegroom as the lover, the desired; the Bridegroom also as he who makes fruitful, the father of children still to be begotten and born. (Certainly the image of a Child in a manger by no means suggests to us a king, giant-killer, bridegroom, and father. But it would not suggest the eternal Word either—if we didn't know. All alike are aspects of the same central paradox.) Then the poet turns to the Bride, with the exhortation, 'forget also thine own people and thy father's house' (11).[3] This sentence has a plain, and to us painful, sense while we read the Psalm as the poet probably intended it. One thinks of home-sickness, of a girl (probably a mere child) secretly crying in a strange *hareem*,[4] of all the miseries which may underlie any dynastic marriage, especially an Oriental one. The poet (who of course knew all about this—he probably had a daughter of his own) consoles her: 'Never mind, you have lost your parents but you will presently have children instead, and children who will be great men.' But all this has also its poignant relevance when the Bride is the Church. A vocation is a terrible thing. … 'Get thee out of thy country, and from thy kindred, and from thy father's house', said God to Abraham (*Genesis* 12, *1*). It is a terrible command; turn your back on all you know. The consolation (if it will at that moment console) is very like that which the Psalmist offers to the bride: 'I will make of thee a great nation.' This 'turn your back' is of course terribly repeated, one may say aggravated, by Our Lord—'he that hateth not father and mother and his own life.'

Reflections on the Psalms (1958), Chapter 12

There are a number of things to be said about this.

Firstly, Lewis assumes that the psalmist was not thinking of Christ at all, merely of a royal marriage. But there are telltale signs in the psalm that the author had a far greater marriage in mind. Addressing the bridegroom King, he writes: 'Your throne, O *God*, is forever and ever' (verse 6). In spite of this, still addressing the bridegroom, he refers to 'your God' in verse 7. The first, in verse 6, is God the Son. The second, in verse 7, is God the Father; Jesus called the Father 'my God' in John 20:17. (The writer of Hebrews noticed all this and used it to prove that Jesus is God in Hebrews 1:8–9.) This does not mean that the psalmist knew as much about the Trinity as we do, but it does mean that he was celebrating a bridegroom who is no less than God. And there is another telltale sign at the end of the psalm. In this part the author is addressing the bride, and he writes: 'I will make your name to be remembered in all generations; Therefore the people shall praise you for ever and ever' (v.17). If the psalmist was thinking only of an ordinary bride for an ordinary king, this would not be true. Clearly he was not. He was thinking of God's own bride, his people.

Therefore, secondly, we can discard Lewis's heart-wrenching picture of a young girl taken to a king's harem against her will. This is not what Psalm 45 is about, thankfully.

Thirdly, Lewis recognises that Christ and his bride the Church are to be seen in this psalm. Although he regards that as the second meaning rather than the first, and although he believed that it was only in God's mind and not in the writer's, at least he does see it. He draws a parallel between verse 10 of the psalm and God's command to Abraham in Genesis 12:1. In this he is quite right; perhaps the psalmist was even deliberately echoing Genesis 12. Abraham was called to make a break with his past, to turn his back on all he knew and set out with God. There is a sense in which each believer, and the Church as a whole, has to do the same. Lewis then goes on, again correctly, to see the same principle in the New Testament. Our Lord claims absolute priority in our lives. Everything else must be rejected in his favour. If a conflict arises, even family must give way to him. All this is hinted at in the psalm.

Concluding comments

In general, Lewis was much more reliable on the New Testament than on the Old. He knew that Christ is the first and central theme of New Testament Scripture, even if he did not grasp that the same is true of the Old Testament. And in fact his writings make much more use of the New than of the Old, as Appendix 3 shows.

His book *Reflections on the Psalms*, though not without its good points, is not a particularly good book. In the hands of a young, inexperienced, or little taught Christian, it could do great harm.

To round off, here are two of Lewis's more worthwhile comments on particular passages of Scripture, together with two other comments.

* * *

1 Corinthians 14:20; Matthew 10:16

... as St Paul points out, Christ never meant that we were to remain children in *intelligence*: on the contrary, He told us to be not only 'as harmless as doves,' but also 'as wise as serpents.' He wants a child's heart, but a grown-up's head. He wants us to be simple, single-minded, affectionate, and teachable, as good children are; but He also wants every bit of intelligence we have to be alert at its job, and in first-class fighting trim. The fact that you are giving money to a charity does not mean that you need not try to find out whether that charity is a fraud or not. The fact that what you are thinking about is God Himself (for example, when you are praying) does not mean that you can be content with the same babyish ideas which you had when you were a five-year-old. It is, of course, quite true that God will not love you any the less, or have less use for you, if you happen to have been born with a very second-rate brain. He has room for people with very little sense, but He wants every one to use what sense they have. The proper motto is not 'Be good, sweet maid, and let who can be clever,' but 'Be good, sweet maid, and don't forget that this involves being as clever as you can.' God is no fonder of intellectual slackers than of any other slackers. If you are thinking of becoming a Christian, I warn you you are embarking on something which is going to take the whole of you, brains and all. But, fortunately, it works the other way round. ...one of the reasons why it needs no special education to be a Christian is that Christianity is an education itself. That is why an uneducated believer like Bunyan was able to write a book that has astonished the whole world.5

Mere Christianity (1952), Book III, Chapter 2

Chapter 6

Luke 14:26

As so often, Our Lord's words are both far fiercer and far more tolerable than those of the theologians. He says nothing about guarding against earthly loves for fear we might be hurt; He says something that cracks like a whip about trampling them all under foot the moment they hold us back from following Him. 'If any man come to me and hate not his father and mother and wife ... and his own life also, he cannot be my disciple' (*Luke* XIV, 26).

But how are we to understand the word *hate*? That Love Himself should be commanding what we ordinarily mean by hatred—commanding us to cherish resentment, to gloat over another's misery, to delight in injuring him—is almost a contradiction in terms. I think Our Lord, in the sense here intended, 'hated' St. Peter when he said, 'Get thee behind me.' To hate is to reject, to set one's face against, to make no concession to, the Beloved when the Beloved utters, however sweetly and however pitiably, the suggestions of the Devil. A man, said Jesus, who tries to serve two masters, will 'hate' the one and 'love' the other. It is not, surely, mere feelings of aversion and liking that are here in question. He will adhere to, consent to, work for, the one and not the other. Consider again, 'I loved Jacob and I *hated* Esau' (*Malachi* I, 2–3). How is the thing called God's 'hatred' of Esau displayed in the actual story? Not at all as we might expect. ...Esau's earthly life was, in every ordinary sense, a good deal more blessed than Jacob's. It is Jacob who has all the disappointments, humiliations, terrors and bereavements. But he has something which Esau has not. He is a patriarch. He hands on the Hebraic tradition, transmits the vocation and the blessing, becomes an ancestor of Our Lord. The 'loving' of Jacob seems to mean the acceptance of Jacob for a high (and painful) vocation; the 'hating' of Esau, his rejection. ...So, in the last resort, we must turn down or disqualify our nearest and dearest when they come between us and our obedience to God. Heaven knows, it will seem to them sufficiently like hatred. We must not act on the pity we feel; we must be blind to tears and deaf to pleadings.

The Four Loves (1960), Chapter 6

...we must sometimes get away from the Authorized Version, if for no other reason, simply *because* it is so beautiful and so solemn. Beauty exalts, but beauty also lulls. Early associations endear but they also confuse. Through that beautiful solemnity the transporting or horrifying realities of which the book tells may come to us blunted and disarmed and we may only sigh with tranquil veneration when we ought to be burning with shame or struck dumb with terror or carried out of ourselves by ravishing hopes and adorations. Does the word 'scourged' really come home to us like 'flogged'? Does 'mocked him' sting like 'jeered at him'?

'Modern Translations of the Bible', 1947

Odd, the way the less the Bible is read the more it is translated.

Letter, 25 May 1962

Notes

1 *The City of God*, Book XVI, Chapter 26.
2 In the small table headed 'Proper psalms on certain days'.
3 Lewis was using the translation of the psalms found in the Book of Common Prayer, by the Reformer Miles Coverdale, which was the one he regularly read. In some psalms the verse numbering is different from the usual, and the verse Lewis quotes here is actually verse 10 in most Bible translations.
4 Lewis puts this in italics because it was still a semi-foreign word at the time, coming from Arabic. This, together with the fact that Arabic uses a different alphabet, also explains Lewis's spelling. The word was not yet English enough to have a normal English spelling, although now the proper spelling is 'harem'.
5 Lewis is referring to John Bunyan's famous book, *The Pilgrim's Progress* (1678, 1684). He loved it.

7 Creation and evolution

In the last chapter we looked at Lewis's view of the Bible. When he went wrong on that, he did so in unusual ways. He was a very independent thinker, and even his mistakes are not often exactly the same as other people's. Because of this we need to be careful that we have grasped what he really thought.

In the same way, his views on creation and evolution are unusual too. He does not quite fit into any of the categories we are used to. In his time, many Christians were happy to admit that evolution was true. Lewis himself thought it was true, sadly, but that is not the whole story. Since his time, Christian opposition to evolution has grown much stronger, and a number of very helpful books have been written on the subject. However, there are still Christians who are prepared to try to combine what the Bible says with evolution. In general terms, Lewis was one of these.

In the first part of this chapter, we will go through various aspects of what the Bible says on the subject, and see where Lewis stood regarding each one of them. That will take the first five sections. Then we will look at some strong criticisms Lewis made of some ideas that are often closely related to evolution. These are dealt with in the last two sections.

In the beginning

'In the beginning God created the heavens and the earth' (Genesis 1:1). In these simple yet profound words, the Bible tells us that everything that exists comes from God. The phrase 'the heavens and the earth' is a way of saying 'everything'. The heavens—everything 'out there', away from the earth; and the earth itself—everything 'down here' on our own planet. All of it had a beginning, and that beginning was when God created it. Only God had no beginning.

On this subject Lewis was about as clear as we could wish. He saw how very different the Bible is from other ideas on this matter. He divided the different ideas people have had into three main categories: the Christian idea of creation, polytheism, and pantheism. Polytheism is the belief that there are many gods, and pantheism is the belief that God and the universe are two aspects of the same thing, without any real distinction between them. Lewis explains:

Some hazy adumbrations of a doctrine of the Fall can be found in Paganism; but it is quite astonishing how rarely outside Christianity we find … a real doctrine of Creation. In Polytheism the gods are usually the product of a universe already in existence… In Pantheism the universe is never something that God made. It is an emanation, something that oozes out of Him, or an appearance, something He looks like to us but really is not, or even an attack of incurable schizophrenia from which He is unaccountably suffering. Polytheism is always, in the long run, nature worship; Pantheism always, in the long run, hostility to nature. None of these beliefs really leaves you free *both* to enjoy your breakfast *and* to mortify your inordinate appetites—much less to mortify appetites recognized as innocent at present lest they should become inordinate.

'Some Thoughts' (1948)

The Christian idea of creation is distinctive in two ways. On the one hand, it is different from polytheism. Polytheism is ancient and was once very widespread. In both Old and New Testament times, the religions of the other nations surrounding Israel were mostly polytheistic (e.g. Exodus 12:12; 1 Samuel 17:43; 2 Chronicles 25:14; 28:23; Acts 14:11–18; 17:16). Today, Hinduism is probably the largest polytheistic religion, and most or all tribal religions are polytheistic. Lewis remarks, 'In Polytheism the gods are usually the product of a universe already in existence.' The Bible begins with God and nothing else. But when polytheistic religions give an account of the beginning, they do not just begin with their gods. Usually or always, there is something else there, either before the gods or perhaps at the same time as one of them, and there is no explanation of how it got there. This means that in polytheism, nature is just as much an ultimate, original thing as the gods are, and sometimes more so. Many of the gods are attached to various aspects of nature. Baal in the Old Testament, for example, was a fertility god, associated with the production of crops. Poseidon was the Greek god of the sea, Thor was the Viking god of thunder. The result, in Lewis's words, is that 'Polytheism is always, in the long run, nature worship'. By contrast, the Bible teaches that God created nature. Nature had a beginning, and is subordinate to him.

But then on the other hand there is pantheism. Pantheism does not have a true idea of creation either, because it does not make a real distinction between creation and the Creator. It ends up in 'hostility to nature' because of what happens when you try to live it out. If you try to live by pantheism, you will sometimes want the god you believe in to give you help (just like everyone else). But 'nature'—the universe in general—will not help you, so you begin to think of it as an obstacle between you and your god.

Lewis was familiar with the world of ideas, and was able to see how distinctive Christianity is in this area. But he was also concerned with the practical consequences of ideas. This is obvious in his last sentence. Christianity recognises that God made the world very good and that much of that goodness remains (Psalm 65:11). This leaves us free to enjoy our breakfasts. But it also teaches that nature, including human nature, is fallen and needs correction. This leaves us the duty of strangling our desires when they go beyond their proper boundaries.

IN SIX DAYS

'In six days the LORD made the heavens and the earth, the sea, and all that is in them' (Exodus 20:11). These words are found in the Fourth Commandment. God commands us to work for six days and rest for one, following the example which he himself set us at creation.

Genesis itself tells us that God created in six days. However, because of modern ideas about evolution, some Christians think that Genesis is not using the word 'day' literally. It may be true that, when the Bible uses that word, it does not always mean a literal twenty-four-hour day (e.g. Ecclesiastes 12:3). (However, there are very, very few clear-cut cases of this out of nearly 1700 uses of the word.) But when it is used in the Fourth Commandment, the word cannot possibly have any meaning other than the usual meaning. God tells us to work for six days because that is exactly what he did. Thankfully, he does not say that he worked for six geological ages and then command us to copy him!

Sadly, Lewis did not believe that the six days recorded in Genesis were simply six days. 'The first chapters of Genesis, no doubt, give the story of creation in the form of a folk-tale', he wrote ('Dogma and the Universe'

[1943]). There is a poem of his called 'The Meteorite', first published in 1946 and reproduced at the beginning of *Miracles* (1947), in which he accepts that the sun existed before the earth:

All that is Earth has once been sky;
Down from the Sun of old she came,
Or from some star that travelled by
Too close to his entangling flame.

Genesis, however, tells us that the sun was only created on the fourth day.

In *Out of the Silent Planet* and *Perelandra*, Lewis assumes that the planets have existed for millions of years. He writes of 'all its millions of years in the unpeopled past' (*Perelandra* [1943], Chapter 12). There is also a reference in *Miracles* to 'pre-human and pre-organic deserts of time' (Chapter 15).

According to their kinds

Genesis tells us that God created each 'kind', or species, of animal individually (1:20–21, 24–25), and mankind individually (vv.26–27). No species is descended from another species; God created each one on its own. We can accept that many variations have arisen *within* particular species. For example, there is an enormous number of dog varieties. But all dogs, however different they are, belong to the same species. What this means is that they can interbreed with one another and produce fertile offspring. No two members of different species can do that.

Evolution, by contrast, asserts that each species has many different species in its ancestry. Over time, it says, species develop variations in such a way that new species actually come into existence out of existing ones. This is what we usually mean when we talk about evolution. It has never been observed happening.

Lewis, however, generally accepted that the history of life on earth has been evolutionary. On many occasions he wrote on the assumption that this was true (for example, Chapter 5 of *The Problem of Pain* [1940]). He believed that evolution is compatible with Christianity. There is a fascinating letter he wrote in reply to Captain Bernard Acworth, a Navy officer who founded the Evolution Protest Movement. We do not know exactly what Acworth wrote, but in his reply Lewis said:

> I am not either attacking or defending Evolution. I believe that Christianity can still be believed, even if Evolution is true. That is where you and I differ. Thinking as I do, I can't help regarding your advice (that I henceforth include arguments against Evolution in all my Christian apologetics) as a temptation to fight the battle on what is really a false issue...
>
> 9 December 1944

This explains why Lewis was happy to write on the assumption that evolution is true. But there is also a trace of something else here. Lewis says that although he is not attacking evolution, he is not defending it either, and that 'Christianity can still be believed, even *if* Evolution is true'. There is a hint here that he did not accept evolution without reservation, and that hint is borne out by things he says elsewhere. The truth is, he knew perfectly well that evolution is a theory that has not been proved. He said that most people believe it with 'a degree of subjective certitude which goes beyond the logical certainty, or even the supposed logical certainty, of the arguments employed' ('Is Theism Important?' [1952]). He regarded it in the same way as the current scientific theory on any other subject: to be accepted provisionally, but in the knowledge that it may well be replaced at some later date (as scientific theories often are).

For this reason, some of his references to evolution show that he did not see it as a definite fact. This comes out very clearly in 'The World's Last Night' (1951):

> I am not in the least concerned to refute Darwinism as a theorem in biology. There may be flaws in that theorem, but I have here nothing to do with them. There may be signs that biologists are already contemplating a withdrawal from the whole Darwinian position, but I claim to be no judge of such signs. It can even be argued that what Darwin really accounted for was not the origin, but the elimination, of species, but I will not pursue that argument. For purposes of this article I am assuming that Darwinian biology is correct.

Adam and Eve

It is not only the Old Testament that speaks of Adam and Eve as real, historical people. The New Testament does so too, in a number of places (they are both mentioned in 1 Timothy 2:13).

It is pleasant to be able to report that the evidence reveals a change of mind by Lewis on this matter. When he wrote *The Problem of Pain* (1940), he regarded it as uncertain how many human beings there were before the Fall. As we have seen, he believed that they were descended from animals. This is what he thought the creation of man might have been like:

For long centuries God perfected the animal form which was to become the vehicle of humanity and the image of Himself. He gave it hands whose thumb could be applied to each of the fingers, and jaws and teeth and throat capable of articulation, and a brain sufficiently complex to execute all the material motions whereby rational thought is incarnated. ... Then, in the fullness of time, God caused to descend upon this organism, both on its psychology and physiology, a new kind of consciousness which could say 'I' and 'me', which could look upon itself as an object, which knew God, which could make judgements of truth, beauty, and goodness, and which was so far above time that it could perceive time flowing past. ...

We do not know how many of these creatures God made, nor how long they continued in the Paradisal state. But sooner or later they fell. Someone or something whispered that they could become as gods ...

(Chapter 5)

It is important for us to notice this idea that 'We do not know how many of these creatures God made'. Elsewhere in *The Problem of Pain* (Chapter 6), and in several letters, Lewis uses the name 'Adam' in a way that could sound as though he believed there literally was a first man called Adam. In the light of his remarks in Chapter 5, however, this is probably not the case. It seems he was only using the name 'Adam' as a kind of shorthand for 'unfallen human beings (however many of them there were)'.

But at some point he changed his mind, and realised that there must have been a literal Adam and Eve. In a letter dated 10 January 1952, he wrote: 'I ... had pictured Adam as being, physically, the son of two anthropoids [man-like animals], on whom, after birth, God worked the miracle which made him Man.' This shows that although he still thought Adam was descended from animals, he did now accept that there was a real first man, and presumably a first woman too.

We do not know exactly when he changed his mind, or why. Many of his references to Adam and Eve could be taken in more than one way. In the Narnia books, for example, the children are sometimes addressed (by Narnians) as 'Son of Adam' or 'Daughter of Eve'. But since this comes in stories it is difficult, without further evidence, to be sure what lies behind it. For what it is worth, I think he changed his mind not long after writing *The Problem of Pain*. In a letter dated 23 December 1941, he mentions that he is writing *Perelandra*, and outlines the plot:

I'm engaged on a sequel to *The Silent Planet* in wh.[ich] the same man goes to Venus. The idea is that Venus is at the Adam-and-Eve stage: i.e. the first two rational creatures have just appeared and are still innocent. My hero arrives in time to prevent their 'falling' as *our* first pair did.

It is just possible that he is only thinking of Adam and Eve here as 'mythical people mentioned in Genesis', but I doubt it. The impact of realising that Adam and Eve were real may even have been one of the things that spurred him into writing *Perelandra*. That is only a guess, but it would be nice to think so. It is certainly a powerful story, one of his own favourites out of all his books.

As to why Lewis changed his mind about Adam and Eve, there is very little evidence indeed. There is, however, one place where he refers to Christ as 'the Second Adam' (a letter dated 8 April 1948). This shows that he had noticed the way the New Testament connects Adam and Christ in Romans 5:12–21 and 1 Corinthians 15:21–22, 45–49. Perhaps that helped him to see that Adam was just as real as Christ himself.

What does it mean to be descended from Adam and Eve? In *Prince Caspian* (1951), Aslan explains to Caspian that, although his family have lived in the Narnian world for many generations, they came originally from our world: ' "You come of the Lord Adam and the Lady Eve," said Aslan. "And that is both honour enough to erect the head of the poorest beggar,

and shame enough to bow the shoulders of the greatest emperor on earth.'"
(Chapter 15).

The Fall

There is *no* relation of any importance between the Fall and Evolution. The doctrine of
Evolution is that organisms have changed, sometimes for what we call (biologically) the
better ... quite often for what we call (biologically) the worse... The doctrine of the Fall
is that at one particular point one species, Man, tumbled down a moral cliff. There is
neither opposition nor support between the two doctrines...

Letter, 1 August 1949

The Bible does not agree with Lewis here. Evolution involves death. It is a
theory about which creatures die sooner than others (among other things).
If evolution had already been going on before the Fall of man, and even
before the creation of man, as Lewis believed, then death was in the world
before the Fall. However, the Bible tells us that 'through one man sin
entered the world, *and death through sin*' (Romans 5:12). When there was
no sin in the world there was no death either; once sin was there death
followed it. Sin and death go together in the Bible. 'The soul who sins shall
die' (Ezekiel 18:4); 'The wages of sin is death' (Romans 6:23).

However, Lewis did know very well that the Fall is foundational in
Christian teaching. Elsewhere he described a different idea as 'wholly
inimical [hostile] to Christianity, for it denies both creation and the Fall'
('Modern Man and his Categories of Thought' [1946]).

In the rest of this chapter we will see Lewis looking at two ways of
thinking which often go alongside evolution, and tackling them head on.

From lower to higher

This, in fact, is the idea Lewis described as 'wholly inimical to
Christianity'. Not many people can describe ideas as well as Lewis could,
so here it is in his own words:

To the modern man it seems simply natural that an ordered cosmos should emerge
from chaos, that life should come out of the inanimate, reason out of instinct,
civilization out of savagery, virtue out of animalism. This idea is supported in his mind

by a number of false analogies: the oak coming from the acorn, the man from the spermatozoon, the modern steamship from the primitive coracle. The supplementary truth that every acorn was dropped by an oak, every spermatozoon derived from a man, and the first boat by something so much more complex than itself as a man of genius, is simply ignored. The modern mind accepts as a formula for the universe in general the principle 'Almost nothing may be expected to turn into almost everything' without noticing that the parts of the universe under our direct observation tell a quite different story.

'Modern Man and his Categories of Thought'

Many ordinary people who believe in evolution probably do have the idea that things in general have got better and better. Biological life has become more and more complex until eventually it produced the human race. Ever since the human race appeared on the scene, our technology has become more and more sophisticated. That is probably a fair summary of many people's ideas about the history of our planet.

Lewis strongly opposed this kind of thinking. Consider his example about boats. Suppose we could travel back in time, beginning with the most sophisticated, best equipped ship of today. Certainly, as we went back, we would find boats becoming less and less sophisticated. Sonar would disappear. Before steel ships we would find iron ships, and before that, wooden ones. They would get smaller too—although the ark would probably not fit that pattern! In general, however, we would find that boats had developed over time. The newer version would usually be the improved version. Thinking along these lines, people get the idea that things in general can be expected to develop from simple to complex over time. But what about when we arrived back at the first boat of all? Where did that come from? It was not a development from something even more simple. Actually, it came from something far more complex—a human brain. Lewis's point is that there is a complex-to-simple movement as well as a simple-to-complex movement.

It is true that we do see all round us things growing up to perfection from small and rude beginnings; but then it is equally true that the small and rude beginnings themselves always come from some full-grown and developed thing. All adults were once babies, true: but then all babies were begotten and borne by adults. Corn does come from seed: but then seed comes from corn.

'Two Lectures', 1945

When people think about evolution, they often have a very strong belief that the history of the world, and even the universe, has been a story of progress from simple to sophisticated. Lewis was careful to say that accepting evolution as a theory in biology does not have to involve believing this. According to real biologists, he thought, not all evolutionary changes have involved increased complexity. He was able to quote one scientist alive at the time, J. B. S. Haldane, to support this idea.[1] Today, however, I think the beliefs of biologists may have changed.

Lewis sometimes called this kind of thinking 'Developmentalism'. Why did he think of it as hostile to Christianity? He explains: '...it is wholly inimical to Christianity, for it denies both creation and the Fall. Where, for Christianity, the Best creates the good and the good is corrupted by sin, for Developmentalism the very standard of good is itself in a state of flux' ('Modern Man and his Categories of Thought').

This raises our last issue.

TOO MUCH EXPLAINING TO DO

As we have seen, Lewis was prepared to accept evolution as a theory in biology. But he did not think it could be the whole story. He was ready to believe that Adam and Eve were descended from animals, but he also believed that it then took a miracle from God to make them human. His idea was that, while human beings are a product of evolution, they are more than a product of evolution. In other words, there are some things about being human that evolution cannot explain. He wrote about two things in particular.

The first thing is our ability to reason. In Chapter 3 of *Miracles* (1947; this chapter was revised in the second edition, 1960), Lewis opposes something he calls 'Naturalism'. This is not the same as evolution, but usually includes it. Naturalism is the name of a position in philosophy. A very good way of finding out what it is would be to read Chapter 2 of *Miracles*, but in trying to sum up that chapter, we could say that

Naturalism is the belief that everything which exists belongs in the same category. Christianity, of course, teaches that God and his creation are in separate categories. The creation is not God, and God does not need his creation. He is not bound to interact with his creation in any particular way; the fact that he does interact with it is simply the result of his free choice. Naturalism, on the other hand, does not believe in such a God. Instead, it believes that everything which exists fits into a huge, interlocking system. Because everything is interlocked, everything is inevitable. Nothing could have turned out any different unless everything had been different right from the beginning. Evolution fits very well in this picture, and probably most of those who believe in Naturalism accept evolution.

How does Naturalism explain the human ability to reason?

> If there is nothing but Nature ... reason must have come into existence by a historical process [Lewis means a process without supernatural intervention]. And of course, for the Naturalist, this process was not designed to produce a mental behaviour that can find truth. There was no Designer... The type of mental behaviour we now call rational thinking or inference must therefore have been 'evolved' by natural selection, by the gradual weeding out of types less fitted to survive.
>
> *Miracles*, Chapter 3

Naturalism has to explain our reasoning power as the result of a cause-and-effect process. And because there was no God on the scene, this process, as Lewis says, 'was not designed to produce a mental behaviour that can find truth'. Finding truth, however, is exactly what human reason has the ability to do. Using reason, a doctor works out exactly what is wrong with a patient, and a detective deduces the identity of a criminal. But since the process that produced reason was not designed to result in this ability—according to Naturalism—it is in that sense accidental. If it is accidental, though, how are we to explain the fact that we can find truth by it? If it was not *designed* to uncover truth, how come it does? That is not really something that can happen accidentally.

'But,' it will be said, 'it is incontestable that we do in fact reach truths by inferences.' Certainly. The Naturalist and I both admit this. We could not discuss anything unless we did. The difference … is that he gives, and I do not, a history of the evolution of reason which is inconsistent with the claims that he and I both have to make for inference as we actually practise it. For his history is, and from the nature of the case can only be, an account, in Cause and Effect terms, of how people came to think the way they do. And this of course leaves in the air the quite different question of how they could possibly be justified in so thinking. This imposes on him the very embarrassing task of trying to show how the evolutionary product which he has described could also be a power of 'seeing' truths.

Miracles, Chapter 3

Evolution cannot explain our ability to arrive at truth by using our reason.

The other thing which evolution cannot explain, and which Lewis wrote about at length, is our knowledge of right and wrong. This takes us back to our last section. Lewis said: 'for Developmentalism the very standard of good is itself in a state of flux'. Christianity, of course, cannot accept a changing standard of what is good and right. The Bible tells us that good and evil are defined by the character of God himself (1 Peter 1:16), and God's character does not change (Malachi 3:6). What is right is always right, and what is wrong is always wrong.

By contrast, many people today believe that there is no such thing as absolute right and wrong. It is not just that they have adopted different standards. Rather, they do not think there are such things as standards, in the Christian sense, at all. Many of these people will still try to live up to the expectations of society. But that is not the same thing as a standard that comes from God himself. For one thing, it does not have absolute authority—it can be broken if there is a good enough reason. For another thing, it can change over time, while God's law never changes (Matthew 5:18–20).

These ideas are clearly opposed to Christianity. But how are they related to evolution? The truth is that if you look at our notions of right and wrong, and then try to explain how evolution has produced these notions in us, you are bound to end up with something like the view just described. If our notions of right and wrong are just a product of evolution, then they cannot have any absolute authority. If our ability to reason is just a product of evolution, it cannot uncover truth about other things; and in the same way, if our sense of right and wrong is a product of evolution, it cannot uncover moral truth. All we are left with is the expectations of society, rather than unchanging truth.

These two things—reason and our moral sense—are closely related. Lewis held to the old view that they are two sides of the same coin, two aspects of our God-given humanity. He even gave our moral sense its old name, 'practical reason', in order to highlight this.

By practical reason I mean our judgment of good and evil. If you are surprised that I include this under the heading of reason at all, let me remind you that your surprise is itself one result of the subjectivism I am discussing. Until modern times no thinker of the first rank ever doubted that our judgments of value were rational judgments [judgments made by reason] or that what they discovered was objective. It was taken for granted that in temptation passion was opposed, not to some sentiment, but to reason. ...The modern view is very different. It does not believe that value judgments are really judgments at all. They are sentiments, or complexes, or attitudes, produced in a community by the pressure of its environment and its traditions, and differing from one community to another. To say that a thing is good is merely to express our feeling about it; and our feeling about it is the feeling we have been socially conditioned to have.

'The Poison of Subjectivism', 1943

Lewis was quite right to say that evolution cannot explain either our reason or our practical reason. He maintained that the principles of both of them must simply be accepted, in their entirety. He put his case most fully in *The Abolition of Man* (1943).

We will end this chapter with a poem in which Lewis makes fun of some of the false ideas we have been looking at.

* * *

Evolutionary Hymn
Lead us, Evolution, lead us
Up the future's endless stair:

Chop us, change us, prod us, weed us.
For stagnation is despair:
Groping, guessing, yet progressing,
Lead us nobody knows where.

Wrong or justice in the present,
Joy or sorrow, what are they
While there's always jam to-morrow,
While we tread the onward way?
Never knowing where we're going,
We can never go astray.

To whatever variation
Our posterity may turn
Hairy, squashy, or crustacean,
Bulbous-eyed or square of stern,
Tusked or toothless, mild or ruthless,
Towards that unknown god we yearn.

Ask not if it's god or devil,
Brethren, lest your words imply
Static norms of good and evil
(As in Plato) throned on high;
Such scholastic, inelastic,
Abstract yardsticks we deny.

Far too long have sages vainly
Glossed great Nature's simple text;
He who runs can read it plainly,
'Goodness = what comes next.'
By evolving, Life is solving
All the questions we perplexed.

Oh then! Value means survival—
Value. If our progeny

Chapter 7

Spreads and spawns and licks each rival,
That will prove its deity
(Far from pleasant, by our present
Standards, though it well may be).

(1957)

Note

1 Haldane wrote: 'We are … inclined to regard progress as the rule in evolution. Actually it is the exception, and for every case of it there are ten of degeneration. It is impossible to define this latter word accurately, but I shall use it to cover cases where an organ or function has been lost without any obvious corresponding gain…' ('Darwinism To-Day' in *Possible Worlds and Other Essays*, 1927). Lewis quotes or refers to this in '*De Futilitate*' (during the Second World War) and 'The Funeral of a Great Myth' (about 1945).

8 Other religions

Another serious error in Lewis's thinking comes in his view of other religions. He believed it was possible for followers of other religions to be saved. He certainly did not believe that all of them would be saved; he knew very well that not all roads lead to God. He also knew that it is our duty to spread the gospel. Nevertheless, he did not think that only Christians go to heaven. He wrote: 'We do know that no man can be saved except through Christ; we do not know that only those who know Him can be saved through Him' (*Mere Christianity* [1952], Book II, Chapter 5).

The second half of that sentence contains a dangerous and troubling mistake. How did Lewis fall into it? To answer that question we need to begin a long way back, with his school days.

Classics

Lewis had been brought up to go to church and to believe that Christianity was true, as many people were at that time. His first serious encounter with other religions was at school, in some of the books he studied. He was introduced to ancient Greek and Roman authors (known as 'the classics'), which in those days was normal. This is how he describes the experience:

Here … one was presented with a mass of religious ideas; and all teachers and editors took it for granted from the outset that these religious ideas were sheer illusion. No one ever attempted to show in what sense Christianity fulfilled Paganism or Paganism prefigured Christianity. The accepted position seemed to be that religions were normally a mere farrago of nonsense, though our own, by a fortunate exception, was exactly true. …the impression I got was that religion in general, though utterly false, was a natural growth, a kind of endemic nonsense into which humanity tended to blunder. In the midst of a thousand such religions stood our own, the thousand and first, labelled True. But on what grounds could I believe in this exception? It obviously was in some general sense the same kind of thing as all the rest. Why was it so differently treated? Need I, at any rate, continue to treat it differently? I was very anxious not to.

Surprised by Joy (1955), Chapter 4

The Greeks and Romans followed pagan religions. Lewis's teachers seemed to think that, while Christianity was entirely true, all other religions were entirely false. This view struck Lewis as extremely unlikely. If there was no truth at all in any of the other religions, why shouldn't he regard Christianity in the same way? And before very long, that was exactly what he did. He became an atheist, although other factors were at work in this as well.

In some respects, these experiences continued to shape his thinking for the rest of his life. We can see already that he was very unlikely ever to accept the view that his teachers put forward; and he never did accept it. When, in later life, he accepted Christianity again, he also accepted that there was some truth in other religions too. In one sense he was right to do so. The apostle Paul tells us: 'when Gentiles, who do not have the law, by nature do the things in the law, these, although not having the law, are a law to themselves, who show the work of the law written in their hearts, their conscience also bearing witness' (Romans 2:14–15). Everyone has a God-given conscience, which makes us aware of right and wrong. Because we are fallen, our consciences can make mistakes, and they are not as sensitive as they should be. Nevertheless, we can expect some awareness of right and wrong even in false religions.

What we cannot expect, however, is an awareness of the gospel. Jesus Christ is the only way to God (John 14:6), but false religions do not present him. A false religion may help a person to understand the problem—sin—but not the answer—Christ. Some religions do recognise the problem to some extent, but can only give wrong answers to it. Lewis was muddled on these matters.

Conversion

Lewis's return to Christianity was bound up with some strange ideas of his own about paganism. When we consider his conversion, we need to try to separate the false elements in his thinking from the genuine work of God—like separating the gold and the dross. In Chapter 2 we looked at the gold; here we must see the dross.

In Chapter 2 we considered a very important letter, written on 18 October 1931, in which Lewis wrote: 'right in the centre of Christianity …

you keep on getting something … very mysterious expressed in those phrases I have so often ridiculed ('propitiation'—'sacrifice'—'the blood of the Lamb') …'. In that letter, he goes on to describe a conversation he had had the previous month with two friends, H. V. D. Dyson and J. R. R. Tolkien:[1]

Now what Dyson and Tolkien showed me was this: that if I met the idea of sacrifice in a Pagan story I didn't mind it at all: again, that if I met the idea of a god sacrificing himself to himself … I liked it very much and was mysteriously moved by it: again, that the idea of the dying and reviving god (Balder, Adonis, Bacchus) similarly moved me provided I met it anywhere *except* in the Gospels. The reason was that in Pagan stories I was prepared to feel the myth as profound and suggestive of meanings beyond my grasp even tho' I could not say in cold prose 'what it meant'.

Now the story of Christ is simply a true myth: a myth working on us in the same way as the others, but with this tremendous difference that *it really happened*: and one must be content to accept it in the same way, remembering that it is God's myth where the others are men's myths: i.e. the Pagan stories are God expressing Himself through the minds of poets, using such images as He found there, while Christianity is God expressing Himself through what we call 'real things'. Therefore it is *true*, not in the sense of being a 'description' of God (that no finite mind could take in) but in the sense of being the way in which God chooses to (or can) appear to our faculties. The 'doctrines' we get *out* of the true myth are of course *less* true: they are translations into our *concepts* and *ideas* of that wh.[ich] God has already expressed in a language more adequate, namely the actual incarnation, crucifixion, and resurrection.

As he says here, Lewis had come to like some pagan myths very much. They appealed to his imagination and emotions. In some of them he thought he saw 'the idea of a god sacrificing himself to himself' and 'the idea of the dying and reviving god', and he liked these ideas. However, when he met somewhat similar ideas in Christianity, he only 'ridiculed' them.

Dyson and Tolkien said that this was inconsistent. They seem to have told their friend that he couldn't have what he wanted both ways. Either he must welcome both the pagan stories and the gospel story too, or neither.

In time, Lewis came round to their way of thinking. He came to believe that these pagan myths had spiritual value, and that Christianity is the fulfilment of them. He knew, of course, as he goes on to say, that the pagan myths do not record historical events and the gospel does. When he calls the gospel story 'a true myth' and 'God's myth', he does not mean that it is not historically true. He means that it is two things at the same time: as well as being true history, it also has the characteristics of myth.

Underlying Lewis's thinking here is a mistake about paganism. This mistake was due to a book he had read called *The Golden Bough* by Sir James George Frazer (published 1890–1915). It was Frazer who thought he saw the idea of a god dying and coming back to life in a number of pagan myths, and Lewis accepted this. However, more recent studies have left Frazer's work out of date. It is so much out of date, in fact, that one writer says: 'There is no unambiguous instance in the history of religion of a dying and rising deity'.[2] The myths themselves bear out this more recent view.

There are two questions we must now ask. Firstly, how did this affect Lewis's thinking about the gospel? Secondly, how did it affect his thinking about paganism?

Attitude to the gospel

Lewis believed that the gospel story is the fulfilment of certain pagan myths, the truth they dimly hinted at. This had two effects on his view of the gospel, one bad and one good.

The bad effect was his attitude to the doctrines of the gospel. We can see this already in the letter quoted above. He says there that the only 'language' good enough to express the gospel is the events themselves—the actual incarnation, crucifixion and resurrection of Christ. When we construct doctrines to express what Christ has done for us, these doctrines are '*less* true', according to Lewis.

It is good to recognise that no single statement can describe the whole of salvation. In fact, all the statements we could possibly make added together would still not be enough to say it all, and this is partly what Lewis means. But he also means that no statement about salvation can be completely accurate, and that is not true. In Chapter 3, we looked at something Lewis says in *Mere Christianity*; here it is again, with the next sentence added:

We are told that Christ was killed for us, that His death has washed out our sins, and that by dying He disabled death itself. That is the formula. That is Christianity. That is what has to be believed. Any theories we build up as to how Christ's death did all this are, in my view, quite secondary: mere plans or diagrams to be left alone if they do not help us, and, even if they do help us, not to be confused with the thing itself.

Book II, Chapter 4

When Lewis talks about 'theories' here, what sort of thing does he have in mind? He gives the following example: 'our being let off because Christ had volunteered to bear a punishment instead of us.' But that is not just a theory—it is a fact. Of course, it does not include everything that could be said about the cross, but what it does say is fully accurate and reliable. Lewis is wrong to call it a theory, and wrong to say that it may help some but not others. He was failing to take such doctrines as seriously as they deserve.

The letter we looked at shows how Lewis fell into this mistake. He describes doctrines as 'translations into our *concepts* and *ideas* of that wh.[ich] God has already expressed in a language more adequate'. Notice the word 'our', meaning our *human* concepts and ideas. This tells us that Lewis is assuming a strong contrast here. On the one hand, he regards the actual events as God's actions—rightly, of course. But on the other hand, he regards the doctrines as having a merely human origin. And this is not right, because they too come from God. In the Bible, God has given us the concepts and ideas he wants us to use in thinking about salvation, and when we do use them, our doctrines come from him.

Lewis's idea that the gospel story fulfilled certain pagan myths had another effect on his attitude to it as well. After his conversion, he was ready to respond to the gospel with his imagination and emotions, just as he responded to the pagan stories (or at least, to Frazer's version of them). He came to the gospel with a wide experience of literature. He had a great gift for appreciating stories of all kinds, and a keen awareness of what makes a good story. He knew that as well as being true, there could not be a better story than the gospel. It stirred his emotions and fired his imagination. The gospel, said Lewis, is 'Perfect Myth and Perfect Fact: claiming not only our love and our obedience, but also our wonder and delight, addressed to the savage, the child, and the poet in each one of us no less than to the moralist, the scholar, and the philosopher' ('Myth Became Fact', 1944).

This, in part, is how he was able to capture so much of the *flavour* of Christianity in his own stories—the Narnia books and his science fiction trilogy. The kind of story Lewis specialised in will not appeal to everyone. But those who have read and enjoyed them have tasted Christianity, whether they realised it or not.

Although we should not adopt Lewis's attitude to paganism, we do need his response of 'wonder and delight' to the gospel story. It is difficult to be sure why we lack it as much as we do. Perhaps the habit of only reading one Bible chapter at a time is preventing us from seeing, and tasting, the story as a whole. Perhaps we concentrate so much on the story of our own lives that the story of Christ's birth, life, death and resurrection drifts into the background. Perhaps we fall into the trap of only thinking about Christ's birth at Christmas and his resurrection at Easter (though the Lord's Supper makes us remember his death more often). There may be many reasons. But surely we cannot deny that we need to feel again and again, like children, the wonder of the greatest story ever told.

Attitude to paganism

What attitude to paganism did Lewis have as a result of his unusual views? Again, there are two things to consider.

Firstly, there are his ideas about God's input into paganism. We came across this matter briefly in Chapter 6 (see p.53). There we saw Lewis thinking that certain pagan stories—stories about 'a god who is killed and broken and then comes to life again'—are part of God's revelation. Just as the Old Testament conveyed the gospel in a shadowy form (Hebrews 10:1), so do these pagan myths, Lewis thought. And already in the letter quoted above, at the very beginning of his Christian life, he describes these stories as 'God expressing Himself through the minds of poets'.

Of course, he did not believe that pagan religions were entirely from God. Elsewhere he wrote: 'in mythology divine and diabolical [from devils] and human elements ... all play a part' (*Reflections on the Psalms* [1958], Chapter 10). The element that he thought came from God was the pattern of a god first dying and then coming back to life. As we saw, Lewis was mistaken in thinking that pagan stories contained this pattern at all. But, following Frazer, he thought they did. Frazer had also thought that this pattern in the myths was a reflection of the same pattern in the crop cycle. Seed falls into the ground and dies, and having died, produces new life when it springs up again. Lewis agreed that the crop cycle was one source of the myths. In many of them, the god was 'almost undisguisedly a personification of the corn', he wrote (*Miracles* [1947], Chapter 14). As a Christian, however, he believed that God had invented the crop cycle. He also believed that God had deliberately designed the crop cycle so as to resemble the death and resurrection of Christ. In this way, Lewis thought, God fully intended the pagans to catch a glimpse of the truth.

With Him there are no accidents. When He created the vegetable world He knew already what dreams the annual death and resurrection of the corn would cause to stir in pious Pagan minds, He knew already that He Himself must so die and live again and in what sense, including and far transcending the old religion of the Corn King, He would say 'This is my Body.'

'Miracles', 1942[3]

Lewis also thought that pagan sacrifices were the result of God's input, at least partly. Here, he is talking about all the various ways in which people claim that God has revealed himself: 'The traditions conflict, yet the longer and more sympathetically we study them the more we become aware of a common element in many of them: the theme of sacrifice, of mystical communion through the shed blood, of death and rebirth, of redemption, is too clear to escape notice' ('Religion Without Dogma?', 1946). The fact that he says 'a common element' and 'the theme', rather than 'common elements' and 'the themes', shows that he regarded all the things he lists here as aspects of a single theme. In Christianity, of course, they are. It is the death and resurrection of Christ that brings us into 'mystical communion' with God. We have 'redemption' through his 'shed blood'. Lewis seems to have imagined that in paganism, too, there was a connection between the myths about a dying and rising god and sacrifices. In reality, however, that connection simply did not exist. Not only were the myths about a dying and rising god not really there at all, pagan sacrifices had little to do with pagan myths.

When the apostle Paul was faced with pagans about to offer sacrifices, he told them to 'turn from these useless things to the living God' (Acts 14:11–15). Paul knew that in the pagan world, God 'did not leave himself without witness' (Acts 14:17). But he did not regard pagan sacrifices as part of this witness to God. The witness God left the pagans was this: 'he did good, gave us rain from heaven and fruitful seasons, filling our hearts with food and gladness' (Acts 14:17). Lewis, however, regarded parts of pagan religion—sacrifices and myths—as a witness to God. This is sad and wrong.

The other thing we need to look at in Lewis's attitude to paganism is his belief that pagans could be saved. He also thought that this was possible for followers of other religions today, as this passage shows:

There are people in other religions who are being led by God's secret influence to concentrate on those parts of their religion which are in agreement with Christianity, and who thus belong to Christ without knowing it. For example, a Buddhist of good will may be led to concentrate more and more on the Buddhist teaching about mercy and to leave in the background (though he might still say he believed) the Buddhist teaching on certain other points. Many of the good Pagans long before Christ's birth may have been in this position.

Mere Christianity (1952), Book IV, Chapter 10

As we saw earlier, other religions do have some glimpses of the truth. They have an awareness of right and wrong (Romans 2:14–15). The Buddhist teaching about mercy would fit into this category. Other religions may agree that we should show mercy to the poor, or that stealing is wrong, or that we should not tell lies. Their moral teachings may be, in Lewis's words, 'in agreement with Christianity'. They do have some grasp of God's moral law, but that is not enough to be saved. 'By the deeds of the law no flesh will be justified in his sight, for by the law is the knowledge of sin' (Romans 3:20). Salvation comes only through the gospel, and other religions contain no trace of the gospel.

This belief of Lewis's comes out in the last of the Narnia books, *The Last Battle* (1956). Here, as in some of the other books, we come across the people of another country in the Narnian world, the Calormenes. The Calormenes worship a false god called Tash. There is a Calormene plot to take over Narnia, and as part of the plot a false religion is invented which mixes up Tash and Aslan, saying that they are the same. Some readers may have been surprised that at this point, Tash himself enters Narnia and is found to be real. However, it is a biblical idea for Tash to be real. Demons are real, and Paul tells us: 'the things which the Gentiles sacrifice they sacrifice to demons and not to God' (1 Corinthians 10:20). When we call false gods 'false', it means that they are not gods; it does not necessarily mean that they are not real. They may be demons. It is no accident that Tash is called a demon in Chapter 8.

There is an unbiblical element in Lewis's story, though. One of the Calormenes finds his way to Aslan's country, heaven. This reflects Lewis's belief that it is possible for followers of other religions to be saved by concentrating on the true parts of their religions. Lewis did not believe that anyone could be saved simply by their own works, apart from Christ. The sentence quoted from *Mere Christianity* at the beginning of this chapter shows that. As we have seen, he thought that the pagan religions contained hints of the gospel, and that it was by such hints that pagans could be saved. I believe the worship of Tash is meant to resemble a pagan religion like that. However, Lewis was mistaken in thinking that such hints were there. It follows that he was also mistaken in thinking that the pagans could have made use of them.

Lewis thought that it was possible for people who have never heard of Christ to be saved by him. But Romans 10:14 tears this view to shreds with a single question: 'How shall they believe in him of whom they have not heard?' According to the Bible this cannot happen. No one can be saved without believing in Christ, and he cannot be believed in where he is not preached.

Lastly, we will pick up on something we looked at earlier in the chapter. We will visit the Narnian world, and find out what happened when Lucy had to read a magician's book.

* * *

Chapter 8

On the next page she came to a spell 'for the refreshment of the spirit'. The pictures were fewer here but very beautiful. And what Lucy found herself reading was more like a story than a spell. It went on for three pages and before she had read to the bottom of the page she had forgotten that she was reading at all. She was living in the story as if it were real, and all the pictures were real too. When she had got to the third page and come to the end, she said, 'That is the loveliest story I've ever read or ever shall read in my whole life. Oh, I wish I could have gone on reading it for ten years. At least I'll read it over again.'

But here part of the magic of the Book came into play. You couldn't turn back. The right-hand pages, the ones ahead, could be turned; the left-hand pages could not.

'Oh, what a shame!' said Lucy. 'I did so want to read it again. Well, at least, I must remember it. Let's see … it was about … about … oh dear, it's all fading away again. And even this last page is going blank. This is a very queer book. How can I have forgotten? It was about a cup and a sword and a tree and a green hill, I know that much. But I can't remember and what *shall* I do?'

And she never could remember; and ever since that day what Lucy means by a good story is a story which reminds her of the forgotten story in the Magician's Book. …

At that moment she heard soft, heavy footfalls coming along the corridor behind her; and of course she remembered what she had been told about the Magician walking in his bare feet and making no more noise than a cat. It is always better to turn round than to have anything creeping up behind your back. Lucy did so.

Then her face lit up … and she ran forward with a little cry of delight and with her arms stretched out. For what stood in the doorway was Aslan himself, the Lion, the highest of all High Kings. And he was solid and real and warm and he let her kiss him and bury herself in his shining mane. And from the low, earthquake-like sound that came from inside him, Lucy even dared to think that he was purring.

'Oh, Aslan,' said she, 'it was kind of you to come.' ...

'Shall I ever be able to read that story again; the one I couldn't remember? Will you tell it to me, Aslan? Oh do, do, do.'

'Indeed, yes, I will tell it to you for years and years. ....'

The Voyage of the Dawn Treader (1952), Chapter 10

Notes

1 Author of *The Lord of the Rings*. Tolkien was a Roman Catholic, something we will look at further in Chapter 9.
2 Jonathan Z. Smith, 'Dying and Rising Gods' *The Encyclopedia of Religion* (Macmillan, 1987).
3 This was a sermon not to be confused with the book of the same name.

9 The world of professing Christianity

In Galatians 2, the apostle Paul describes how he once had to confront the apostle Peter. Under pressure from a number of fellow Jewish Christians, Peter had 'separated himself' from Gentile Christians, refusing to eat with them (Galatians 2:12). This means that Peter had been affected by the view recorded in Acts 15:5: 'It is necessary to circumcise them, and to command them to keep the law of Moses.' Some people were saying that when Gentiles became Christians, they had to be circumcised and keep Old Testament laws such as the food laws. In effect, they thought that Gentiles could only become Christians if they became Jews as well.

Paul took this very seriously. He told Peter: 'you compel Gentiles to live as Jews' (Galatians 2:14). This was because Peter was keeping himself separate from Gentile Christians *unless* they had been circumcised and kept the Old Testament laws. Of course, since Peter was an apostle, this put a lot of pressure on the Gentiles to do just that.

The reason Paul took this so seriously is that it was not just a question of lifestyle. The gospel itself was under threat. 'A man is not justified by the works of the law but by faith in Jesus Christ' (Galatians 2:16). Nothing that we do can justify us before God, and that includes keeping Old Testament food laws. But Peter, by his actions, was giving the impression that you couldn't be a Christian unless you did that. He made it look as if faith by itself was not enough. The doctrine of justification by faith alone was at stake. And *Peter*, an apostle of Jesus Christ, was unclear about it!

This all took place in the church at Antioch (Galatians 2:11). Peter was not alone. 'The rest of the Jews'—that is, Jewish Christians—acted in the same way (Galatians 2:13). We can sense Paul's shock and sadness as he recalls, 'even Barnabas was carried away with their hypocrisy' (Galatians 2:13). When Barnabas first came across large numbers of Gentile Christians, which happened in Antioch, 'he was glad' (Acts 11:20–23). Together with Paul, he had taught the church there 'for a whole year' (Acts

11:25–26). It was in Antioch at that time that believers, both Jewish and Gentile, 'were first called Christians' (Acts 11:26). Yet now even Barnabas had caved in. Once he had loved, taught and encouraged the Gentile Christians of Antioch. Now he refused to have fellowship with them.

What a crisis moment! Paul's response to Peter was daring but needed: 'I withstood him to his face, because he was to be blamed' (Galatians 2:11).

Why was Paul writing about all this to the Galatian churches? Because they were wavering on the very same issue. They were not clear about the doctrine of justification by faith alone. It is this doctrine that Paul was striving to teach them. It is possible, then, for a real Christian to be unclear about this. There may well have been some people in the Galatian churches who were not really Christians at all. Equally, however, there were many people who were. Peter and Barnabas, too, were certainly Christians.

This was also the position of C. S. Lewis. There is a difference between asking, 'Did Lewis fully understand the doctrine of justification by faith alone?' and asking, 'Did Lewis himself trust in Christ alone for justification?' Even though we have to answer 'no' to the first question, we can still answer 'yes' to the second. At one stage that was true of an apostle. Surely we can admit that it was true of Lewis as well.

Faith and works

Actually, there was not much confusion about this in Lewis's thinking, though there was a little. He firmly opposed the idea that we can earn God's favour in a number of places. Here is one example:

The main thing we learn from a serious attempt to practise the Christian virtues is that we fail. If there was any idea that God had set us a sort of exam. and that we might get good marks by deserving them, that has to be wiped out. If there was any idea of a sort of bargain—any idea that we could perform our side of the contract and thus put God in our debt so that it was up to Him, in mere justice, to perform His side—that has to be wiped out.

I think every one who has some vague belief in God, until he becomes a Christian, has the idea of an exam. or of a bargain in his mind. The first result of real Christianity is to blow that idea into bits.

Mere Christianity (1952), Book III, Chapter 11

Chapter 9

Yet, in the very next chapter, Lewis seems to be saying something very different: 'Christians have often disputed as to whether what leads the Christian home is good actions, or Faith in Christ. I have no right really to speak on such a difficult question, but it does seem to me like asking which blade in a pair of scissors is most necessary' (Book III, Chapter 12).

At first sight these words are alarming. However, notice that the phrase 'what leads the Christian home' is vague. It is not as if Lewis had written, 'what wins us God's approval'. That would have been far more definite and would have given us grave cause for concern. As things are, we need to find out from the rest of these two chapters what he means.

When we do that, we find that he is writing on the basis of his own experience of becoming a Christian. In Chapter 2, we saw that he spent a long time trying to make himself live up to God's standards. In the end he was driven to admit that he could not do so, and threw himself on Christ instead.

He remembered this experience all his life. His struggle to make himself holy had ended in failure. He felt, too, that if he had not struggled he would not have realised his failure. It was his efforts to find righteousness in himself that had shown him his sin and need so clearly. In turn, this realisation had driven him to Christ.

As a result, he thought that such an experience was an essential part of becoming a Christian. When he writes, in *Mere Christianity*, that good works are 'necessary', we must ask what he thought them necessary *for*. The answer is: For making us realise that our own efforts can never make us good enough. That is why, for example, he writes:

… as long as a man is thinking of God as an examiner who has set him a sort of paper to do, or as the opposite party in a sort of bargain—as long as he is thinking of claims and counter-claims between himself and God—he is not yet in the right relation to Him. He is misunderstanding what he is and what God is. And he cannot get into the right relation until he has discovered the fact of our bankruptcy.

When I say 'discovered', I mean really discovered: not simply said it parrot-fashion. … really finding out by experience that it is true.

Now we cannot, in that sense, discover our failure to keep God's law except by trying our very hardest (and then failing). Unless we really try, whatever we say there will always be at the back of our minds the idea that if we try harder next time we shall succeed in being completely good. Thus, in one sense, the road back to God is a road of moral effort, of trying harder and harder. But in another sense it is not trying that is ever going to bring us home. All this trying leads up to the vital moment at which you turn to God and say, 'You must do this. I can't.'

Book III, Chapter 12

Lewis does make a mistake here, but it is not the fatal mistake of thinking that our good works can help win God's approval. His real mistake is to regard the way it was for him as the way it must be for everyone else. Some things are the same in every conversion, but other things vary from person to person. As we saw in Chapter 2, Lewis discovered a great deal about his own sinfulness *before* he became a Christian. In this he was unusual. The very fact that he tried so hard to make himself holy gave him an unusually clear awareness of his sin.

Of course, none of us became Christians without some awareness of our own sin. But we did not all have this awareness to the same extent. It is possible to trust in Christ without having seen nearly as much of our sin as Lewis did. We then come to see more of it *after* our conversion—as, indeed, every Christian does.

Lewis also made another mistake which is related to the matter of faith and works.

'Mere Christianity'

The Roman Catholic church teaches that we cannot be justified by faith alone. This is not the place to take a detailed look at the official Roman Catholic teaching, but briefly, it defines justification wrongly. Its teaching on this contradicts the gospel itself, and has serious consequences for many of its other teachings. The total effect, on very many of its followers, is to make them think that God's acceptance of them depends on their own actions. In this way it leads millions astray. We may hope that a few Roman Catholics, here and there, have been led to trust in Christ alone. But the vast majority clearly trust in their church, and in the actions that it encourages them to perform, rather than in Christ.[1]

Lewis, however, was happy to regard Roman Catholics as fellow-Christians. This was partly because his grasp of the true doctrine of justification was not entirely clear, but partly also because he did not fully understand the Catholic stance on this doctrine. Nevertheless, it is unhelpful to find in his writings that he thought of Catholics as true Christians. Many Christians today have not been warned about the great dangers of Catholicism. For them, it is all too easy to regard disapproval of it as just an old prejudice. Of course, Protestants often have been prejudiced against Catholics, but there are biblical reasons for disapproval too. Lewis's stance does not help those who have not realised this.

Lewis thought it was a shame that there are so many different Christian denominations. He regarded the Roman Catholic church as one of them, of course. In his book *Mere Christianity*, he aimed to defend what was common to them all. The title reflects this: he wanted to introduce people, not to Anglican Christianity, or Baptist Christianity, but to mere *Christianity*. He took this title from the seventeenth-century pastor Richard Baxter.[2]

In the same year in which *Mere Christianity* was published, Lewis made the following statement about the Church of England in a letter to *Church Times*:

…what unites the Evangelical and the Anglo-Catholic against the 'Liberal' or 'Modernist' is something very clear and momentous, namely, the fact that both are thoroughgoing supernaturalists, who believe in the Creation, the Fall, the Incarnation, the Resurrection, the Second Coming, and the Four Last Things.[3] …

The point of view from which this agreement seems less important than their divisions, or than the gulf which separates both from any non-miraculous version of Christianity, is to me unintelligible. Perhaps the trouble is that as supernaturalists … thus taken together, they lack a name. May I suggest … Baxter's 'mere Christians'?

printed 8 February 1952

Lewis is right, of course, to say that all the beliefs he mentions here are very important. In fact, he implies that 'liberals' who do not agree with them are not Christians at all. If those who do hold these beliefs are to be regarded as 'mere Christians', it follows that those who do not hold them are not. Yet

Lewis clearly did not think that the doctrine of justification had the same importance. He would never have dreamed of saying that certain people were not Christians simply because of their beliefs about that. Sadly, there are those in the Church of England today who are called evangelicals, but who seem to be taking the very position that Lewis outlines here.

Agreements and disagreements

We should note that Lewis did have strong objections to various features of Roman Catholicism. Since he regarded Roman Catholics as Christians, it is understandable that he was unwilling to voice these objections in public. Very occasionally, however, he was drawn to express them in private letters. Here is a particularly clear example:

What is most certain is the vast mass of doctrine wh.[ich] I find agreed on by Scripture, the Fathers, the Middle Ages, modern R.C.'s, modern Protestants. That is true 'catholic'4 doctrine. Mere 'modernism' I reject at once.

The Roman Church where it differs from this universal tradition and specially from apostolic Xtianity I reject. Thus their theology about the B.[lessed] V.[irgin] M.[ary] I reject because it seems utterly foreign to the New Testament: where indeed the words 'Blessed is the womb that bore thee' receive a rejoinder pointing in exactly the opposite direction [Luke 11:27–28]. Their papalism seems equally foreign to the attitude of St Paul towards St Peter in the Epistles [i.e., in Galatians 2]. The doctrine of Transubstantiation insists on defining in a way wh.[ich] the N.T. seems to me not to countenance. In a word, the whole set-up of modern Romanism seems to me to be as much a provincial or local *variation* from the central, ancient tradition as any particular Protestant sect is.

8 May 1945

At the same time, Lewis was certainly capable of taking on board rather too much from other branches of professing Christianity. We came across one example of this in Chapter 4, when we considered his views on the use of statues and pictures in worship. While he gave a perceptive account of their dangers, he was still willing to believe that they have their place for some people.

Another striking example is that he believed in purgatory. We may find this surprising, and it is certainly wrong. But we can understand it if we see it in the right light.

Roman Catholics believe that most Christians do not go straight to heaven when they die. Instead, they believe that they go for a time to a place of suffering called purgatory. According to Catholicism this serves two purposes: it punishes them for sins, and purifies them from sin. There is no evidence that Lewis agreed about the first, but he did agree about the second. All through our Christian lives, God is sanctifying us, making us more holy. But it is obvious that this process is still not complete by the time we die. Lewis believed that it is completed *after* death, in purgatory.

Our souls *demand* Purgatory, don't they? Would it not break the heart if God said to us, 'It is true, my son, that your breath smells and your rags drip with mud and slime, but we are charitable here and no one will upbraid you with these things, nor draw away from you. Enter into the joy.'? Should we not reply, 'With submission, sir, and if there is no objection, I'd *rather* be cleaned first.' 'It may hurt, you know'—'Even so, sir.'

I assume that the process of purification will normally involve suffering. Partly from tradition; partly because most real good that has been done me in this life has involved it.

Letters to Malcolm: Chiefly on Prayer (1964), 20

In order to understand why he thought this, we need to know exactly what we ought to believe instead. There is a belief missing from Lewis's thinking here. It is only if we grasp it ourselves that we will be able to understand the whole matter. The missing belief is this: that we are made completely holy the moment we die.

The Bible never mentions purgatory. It makes it very clear that when Christians die they go straight to heaven. Jesus said to the dying thief, '...*today* you will be with me in paradise' (Luke 23:43, my italics). Paul knew that 'to be absent from the body' means 'to be present with the Lord' (2 Corinthians 5:8). But this only makes sense if believers are free from all sin as soon as they die. How else could we be allowed into God's holy presence? 'The spirits of just men' have been 'made perfect' (Hebrews 12:23). That is what Lewis had not realised. But it is a truth that is full of comfort for us, and we must remember it. When Lewis lost his wife, an extra strand of distress was woven into his grief because he believed she was in purgatory. It is pitiable to find him writing:

How do I know that all her anguish is past? I never believed before—I thought it immensely improbable—that the faithfullest soul could leap straight into perfection and peace the moment death has rattled in the throat. It would be wishful thinking with a vengeance to take up that belief now. H.[5] was a splendid thing; a soul straight, bright, and tempered like a sword. But not a perfected saint. A sinful woman married to a sinful man; two of God's patients, not yet cured. I know there are not only tears to be dried but stains to be scoured. The sword will be made even brighter.

But oh God, tenderly, tenderly. Already, month by month and week by week you broke her body on the wheel whilst she still wore it. Is it not yet enough?

A Grief Observed (1961), Chapter 3

But perhaps his own entrance into glory was especially sweet.

* * *

Conversion requires an alteration of the will, and an alteration which, in the last resort, does not occur without the intervention of the supernatural.

'The Decline of Religion', 1946.

It is not enough to want to get rid of one's sins. We also need to believe in the One who saves us from our sins. Not only do we need to recognise that we are sinners; we need to believe in a Saviour who takes away sin.

'Cross-Examination', 1963.

Notes

1 The Roman Catholic position on justification is explained and answered by Philip H. Eveson, Chapter 7, *The Great Exchange* (Epsom: Day One Publications, 1996).

2 The relevant passage from Baxter is quoted in Roger Lancelyn Green and Walter Hooper,

C. S.Lewis: a Biography (revised edition, HarperCollins, 2002), p. 247. Baxter makes it clear that he is not including Roman Catholics.

3   This is a traditional expression which refers to death, judgement, heaven and hell.

4   The original meaning of the word 'catholic' is 'universal'.

5   'H' is for his wife's first name, Helen, though she was usually known by her second name, Joy.

1 Some glimpses of wisdom

This is a collection of 'Lewis quotes' on a wide range of subjects not dealt with elsewhere in this book. Browse, and find subject after subject lit up by his God-given wisdom!
For ease of use, sources are listed at the end of the chapter (pp. 107).

... the trouble about trying to make yourself stupider than you really are is that you very often succeed.

I am a democrat because I believe in the Fall of Man. I think most people are democrats for the opposite reason. A great deal of democratic enthusiasm descends from the ideas of people like Rousseau, who believed in democracy because they thought mankind so wise and good that everyone deserved a share in the government. The danger of defending democracy on those grounds is that they're not true. And whenever their weakness is exposed, the people who prefer tyranny make capital out of the exposure. I find that they're not true without looking further than myself. I don't deserve a share in governing a hen-roost, much less a nation. Nor do most people—all the people who believe advertisements, and think in catchwords and spread rumours. The real reason for democracy is just the reverse. Mankind is so fallen that no man can be trusted with unchecked power over his fellows.

The process of being brought up, however well it is done, cannot fail to offend.

'Creation' as applied to human authorship ... seems to me an entirely misleading term. ...we re-arrange elements He has provided. There is not a *vestige* of real creativity ... in us. Try to imagine a new primary colour, a third sex, a fourth dimension, or even a monster wh[ich]. does not consist of bits of existing animals stuck together! Nothing happens. ...

Writing a book is much less like creation than it is like planting a garden or begetting a child: in all three cases we are only entering as *one* cause into a causal stream which works, so to speak, in its own way. I w[oul]d. not wish it to be otherwise. If one c[oul]d. *really* create in the strict sense w[oul]d. one not find one had created a sort of Hell?

It has always seemed to me odd that those who are sent to evangelise the Bantus begin by learning Bantu while the Church turns out annually curates to teach the English who simply don't know the vernacular language of England...

All joy (as distinct from mere pleasure, still more amusement) emphasises our pilgrim status: always reminds, beckons, awakes desire. Our best havings are wantings.

... I never had the experience of looking for God. It was the other way round; He was the hunter (or so it seemed to me) and I was the deer. He stalked me like a redskin, took unerring aim, and fired. And I am very thankful that that is how the first (conscious) meeting occurred. It forearms one against subsequent fears that the whole thing was only wish fulfilment. Something one didn't wish for can hardly be that.

'Aslan,' said Lucy, you're bigger.'

'That is because you are older, little one,' answered he.

'Not because you are?'

'I am not. But every year you grow, you will find me bigger.'

It must always *sound* like real conversation but must be in reality clearer and more economical than that. Literature is an art of *illusion*.

The moment one asks oneself 'Do I believe?' all belief seems to go. I think this is because one is trying to turn round and look *at* something which is there to be used and work *from*—trying to take out one's eyes instead of keeping them in the right place and seeing *with* them. I find that it happens about other matters as well as faith. In my experience only v. robust pleasures will stand the question, 'Am I really enjoying this?'... St Paul speaks of 'Faith actualised in Love' [Galatians 5:6].

I think that if God forgives us we must forgive ourselves. Otherwise it is almost like setting up ourselves as a higher tribunal than him.

I would prefer to combat the 'I'm special' feeling not by the thought 'I'm no more special than anyone else', but by the feeling 'Everyone is as special as me'. In one way there is no difference, I grant, for both remove the speciality. But there is a difference in another way. The first might lead you to think, 'I'm only one of the crowd like everyone else'. But the second leads to the truth that there isn't any crowd. No one is like anyone else. All are 'members' (organs) in the Body of Christ. All different and all necessary to the whole and to one another: each loved by God individually... Otherwise you might get the idea that God is like the government which can only deal with the people in the mass.

We outgrow youth far sooner than childhood.

We must attack the enemy's line of communication. What we want is not more little books about Christianity, but more little books by Christians on other subjects—with their Christianity *latent*. You can see this most easily if you look at it the other way round. Our Faith is not very likely to be shaken by any book on Hinduism. But if whenever we read an elementary book on Geology, Botany, Politics or Astronomy, we found that its implications were Hindu, that would shake us. It is not the books written in direct defence of Materialism that make the modern man a materialist; it is the materialistic assumptions in all the other books. In the same way, it is not books on Christianity that will really trouble him. But he would be troubled if, whenever he wanted a cheap popular introduction to some science, the best work on the market was always by a Christian.

'Daughter,' said the Hermit, 'I have now lived a hundred and nine winters in this world and have never yet met any such thing as Luck...'.

When I have learnt to love God better than my earthly dearest, I shall love my earthly dearest better than I do now. In so far as I learn to love my earthly dearest at the expense of God and *instead* of God, I shall be moving towards the state in which I shall not love my earthly dearest at all.

I think what makes even beautiful country (in the long run) so unsatisfactory when seen from a train or a car is that it whirls each tree, brook, or haystack close up into the foreground, *soliciting* individual attention but vanishing before you can give it ...

Yes. I know one doesn't even *want* to be cured of one's pride because it gives pleasure.

But the pleasure of pride is like the pleasure of scratching. If there is an itch one does want to scratch: but it is much nicer to have *neither* the itch nor the scratch. As long as we have the itch of self-regard we shall want the pleasure of self-approval: but the happiest moments are those when we forget our precious selves and have neither but have everything else (God, our fellow humans, animals, the garden and the sky) instead ...

The emotional effect of music may be not only a distraction (to some people at some times) but a delusion: i.e. feeling certain emotions in church they mistake them for religious emotions when they may be wholly natural.

... about Punishment. The modern view, by excluding the retributive element and concentrating solely on deterrence and cure, is hideously immoral. It is vile tyranny to submit a man to compulsory 'cure' or sacrifice him to the deterrence of others, unless he *deserves* it.

Lucy could only say, 'It would break your heart.' 'Why,' said I, 'was it so sad?' 'Sad!! No,' said Lucy.

(1) Always try to use the language so as to make quite clear what you mean and make sure your sentence couldn't mean anything else.

(2) Always prefer the plain direct word to the long, vague one. Don't *implement* promises, but *keep* them.

(3) Never use abstract nouns when concrete ones will do. If you mean 'more people died' don't say 'mortality rose'.

(4) In writing. Don't use adjectives which merely tell us how you want us to *feel* about the thing you are describing. I mean, instead of telling us a thing was 'terrible', describe it so that we'll be terrified. Don't say it was 'delightful': make *us* say 'delightful' when we've read the description. You see, all those words (horrifying, wonderful, hideous, exquisite) are only like saying to your readers 'Please will you do my job for me'.

(5) Don't use words too big for the subject. Don't say 'infinitely' when you mean 'very';

otherwise you'll have no word left when you want to talk about something *really* infinite ...

Lady, a better sculptor far
Chiselled those curves you smudge and mar,
And God did more than lipstick can
To justify your mouth to man.

Someone becomes a Christian, or, in a family nominally Christian already, does something like becoming a missionary ... The others suffer a sense of outrage. What they love is being taken from them! The boy must be mad! And the conceit of him! Or is there something in it after all? Let's hope it is only a phase! If only he'd listen to his natural advisers! Oh come back, come back, be sensible, be the dear son we used to know. Now I, as a Christian, have a good deal of sympathy with these jealous, puzzled, suffering people (for they do suffer and out of their suffering much of the bitterness against religion arises). I believe the thing is common. There is very nearly a touch of it in Luke II, 48, 'Son, *why hast thou* so dealt with us?' And is the reply easy for a loving heart to bear?

I am ... far from agreeing with those who think all religious fear barbarous and degrading and demand that it should be banished from the spiritual life. Perfect love, we know, casteth out fear [1 John 4:18]. But so do several other things—ignorance, alcohol, passion, presumption, and stupidity. It is very desirable that we should all advance to that perfection of love in which we shall fear no longer; but it is very undesirable, until we have reached that stage, that we should allow any inferior agent to cast out our fear.

... we must be very cautious of snatching at any scientific theory which, for the moment, seems to be in our favour. We may *mention* such things; but we must mention them lightly and without claiming that they are more than 'interesting'. Sentences beginning 'Science has now proved' should be avoided. If we try to base our apologetic on some recent development in science, we shall usually find that just as we have put the finishing touches to our argument science has changed its mind and quietly withdrawn the theory we have been using as our foundation stone.

... the content of the newspapers ... is possibly the most phantasmal of all histories ...

I cannot offer you a water-tight technique for awaking the sense of sin. I can only say that, in my experience, if one begins from the sin that has been one's own chief problem during the last week, one is very often surprised at the way this shaft goes home. But whatever method we use, our continual effort must be to get their minds away from public affairs and 'crime' and bring them down to brass tacks—to the whole network of spite, greed, envy, unfairness and conceit in the lives of 'ordinary decent people' like themselves (and ourselves).

'Grown-up, indeed,' said the Lady Polly. 'I wish she *would* grow up. She wasted all her school time wanting to be the age she is now, and she'll waste all the rest of her life trying to stay that age. Her whole idea is to race on to the silliest time of one's life as quick as she can and then stop there as long as she can.'

I have found that nothing is more dangerous to one's own faith than the work of an apologist. No doctrine of that Faith seems to me so spectral, so unreal as one that I have just successfully defended in a public debate. For a moment, you see, it has seemed to rest on oneself: as a result, when you go away from that debate, it seems no stronger than that weak pillar.

Does not every movement in the Passion write large some common element in the sufferings of our race? First, the prayer of anguish; not granted. Then He turns to His friends. They are asleep—as ours, or we, are so often, or busy, or away, or preoccupied. Then He faces the Church; the very Church that He brought into existence. It condemns Him. This is also characteristic. In every Church, in every institution, there is something which sooner or later works against the very purpose for which it came into existence. But there seems to be another chance. There is the State; in this case, the Roman state. Its pretensions are far lower than those of the Jewish church, but for that very reason it may be free from local fanaticisms. It claims to be just, on a rough, worldly level. Yes, but only so far as is consistent with political expediency and *raison d'état*. One becomes a counter in a complicated game. But even now all is not lost. There is still an appeal to the People—the poor and simple whom He had blessed, whom He had healed and fed and taught, to whom He himself belongs. But they have become over-night (it is nothing unusual) a murderous rabble shouting for His blood. There is, then, nothing left but God. And to God, God's last words are, 'Why hast thou forsaken me?'

... the pestilent notion ... that each of us starts with a treasure called 'personality' locked up inside him, and that to expand and express this, to guard it from interference, to be 'original', is the main end of life. ...No man who values originality will ever be original. But try to tell the truth as you see it, try to do any bit of work as well as it can be done for the work's sake, and what men call originality will come unsought.

When we merely *say* that we are bad, the 'wrath' of God seems a barbarous doctrine; as soon as we *perceive* our badness, it appears inevitable, a mere corollary from God's goodness.

For my own part, I tend to find the doctrinal books often more helpful in devotion than the devotional books, and I rather suspect that the same experience may await many others. I believe that many who find 'nothing happens' when they sit down, or kneel down, to a book of devotion, would find that the heart sings unbidden while they are working their way through a tough bit of theology...

A serious attempt to repent and really to know one's sins is in the long run a lightening and relieving process. Of course, there is bound to be at first dismay and often terror and later great pain, yet that is much less in the long run than the anguish of a mass of unrepented and unexamined sins, lurking in the background of our minds. It is the difference between the pain of the tooth about which you should go the dentist and the simple straightforward pain which you know is getting less and less every moment when you have had the tooth out.

Man is becoming as narrowly 'practical' as the irrational animals. In lecturing to popular audiences I have repeatedly found it almost impossible to make them understand that I recommended Christianity because I thought its affirmation to be objectively *true*. They are simply not interested in the question of truth or falsehood. They only want to know if it will be comforting, or 'inspiring', or socially useful.

... the Head's friends saw that the Head was no use as a Head, so they got her made an Inspector to interfere with other Heads. And when they found she wasn't much good even at that, they got her into Parliament where she lived happily ever after.

Friends are not primarily absorbed in each other. It is when we are doing things together that friendship springs up—painting, sailing ships, praying, philosophising, fighting shoulder to shoulder. Friends look in the same direction. Lovers look at each other, that is, in opposite directions.

He demands our worship, our obedience, our prostration. Do we suppose that they can do Him any good …? A man can no more diminish God's glory by refusing to worship Him than a lunatic can put out the sun by scribbling the word 'darkness' on the walls of his cell. But God wills our good, and our good is to love Him (with that responsive love proper to creatures) and to love Him we must know Him: and if we know Him, we shall in fact fall on our faces.

And have you ever noticed what a fine line, crossed in a split second, separates the snugness of privacy from the vacuity of loneliness? You glance round the room—all the same, but all changed.

(1) Turn off the Radio.

(2) Read all the good books you can, and avoid nearly all magazines.

(3) Always write (and read) with the ear, not the eye. You sh[oul]d hear every sentence you write as if it was being read aloud or spoken. If it does not sound nice, try again.

(4) Write about what really interests you, whether it is real things or imaginary things, and nothing else. (Notice this means that if you are interested *only* in writing you will never be a writer, because you will have nothing to write about….)

(5) Take great pains to be *clear*. Remember that though you start by knowing what you mean, the reader doesn't, and a single ill-chosen word may lead him to a total misunderstanding. In a story it is terribly easy just to forget that you have not told the reader something that he needs to know—the whole picture is so clear in your own mind that you forget that it isn't the same in his.

(6) When you give up a bit of work don't (unless it is hopelessly bad) throw it away. Put it in a drawer. It may come in useful later. Much of my best work, or what I think my best, is the rewriting of things begun and abandoned years earlier.

(7) Don't use a typewriter. The noise will destroy your sense of rhythm, which still needs years of training.

(8) Be sure you know the meaning (or meanings) of every word you use.

If there is Providence at all, everything is providential and every providence is a special providence.

'Logic!' said the Professor half to himself. 'Why don't they teach logic at these schools? …'

Sources

P.99
The Magician's Nephew (1955), Chapter 10
'Equality', 1943
'The Funeral of a Great Myth', uncertain date
Letter, 20 February 1943
P.100
Letter, 7 October 1945
Letter, 5 November 1954
'The Seeing Eye', 1963
Prince Caspian (1951), Chapter 10
Letter, 31 August 1948
Letter, 27 September 1949
Letter, 19 April 1951
Letter, 20 June 1952
P.101
Letter, 3 March 1943
'Christian Apologetics', 1945
The Horse and his Boy (1954), Chapter 10
Letter, 8 November 1952
Letter, 9 January 1954
Letter, 18 February 1954

Appendix 1

P.102

Letter, March 1956

Letter, 25 May 1962

The Voyage of the Dawn Treader (1952), Chapter 16

Letter, 26 June 1956

P.103

Poems (1964)

Letter, 10 February 1957

'The World's Last Night', 1951

'Christian Apologetics', 1945

'Historicism', 1950

P.104

'Christian Apologetics', 1945

The Last Battle (1956), Chapter 12

'Christian Apologetics', 1945

Letters to Malcolm: Chiefly on Prayer (1964), 8

P.105

'Membership', 1945

The Problem of Pain (1940), Chapter 4

'On the Reading of Old Books', 1944

'Miserable Offenders', 1946

'Modern Man and his Categories of Thought', 1946

The Silver Chair (1953), Chapter 16

'Equality', 1943

P.106

The Problem of Pain (1940), Chapter 3

Letter, 3rd February 1940

Letter, 14 December 1959

P.107

Letters to Malcolm: Chiefly on Prayer (1964), 10

The Lion, the Witch and the Wardrobe (1950), Chapter 5

2 A chronological list of the works of C. S. Lewis

L ists of Lewis's works have appeared before. This one differs from those I have seen in two main ways:

(1) Previous lists have divided different kinds of work into different sections—books, articles, poems, reviews, etc. In this list everything is given together.

(2) Previous lists have placed items not published till after Lewis's death under the date of their publication. In this list, these items are placed under the date of composition, delivery, etc. The only exceptions to this are items that he prepared for publication before his death but which did not actually appear till after it. These are Nos. 454, 458–460, and I presume 453.

The aim of these features is to give an even clearer idea of the astonishingly large and varied output which Lewis maintained almost throughout his life.

In some cases the title given is not the title under which the item was first published. I thought it more useful to give the title by which it would generally be known now.

Where 'Boxen' occurs in brackets I have assumed that Lewis produced Boxonian material that has not survived.

Many of the poems in *Poems* (1964) were previously published elsewhere. Apart from those in *The Pilgrim's Regress* (1933) these are also listed separately. Some of these (if not all of them) were revised later.

The Guardian in this list is an extinct Church of England newspaper.

Letters published in Lewis's lifetime (in journals, etc.) are listed individually.

I have not included comments by Lewis on other people's books, which sometimes appeared on their covers, with the exception of No. 398 because that has been published separately since.

Only UK publications appear here.

Under each year, items for which we know only the year appear at the end of the list (along with the letters, which of course are not listed individually).

Undetermined date

1 'The Man Born Blind'—late 1920s according to his close friend Owen Barfield.
2 'Launcelot'—probably 1930s.
3 'The Queen of Drum'—not later than 1938; Lewis's friend and posthumous editor Walter Hooper guesses 1933–34.
4 *The Dark Tower* (unfinished) 1939 or 1940.
5 'Tasso'—judged 1940s by Hooper.
6 'On Ethics'—probably preceded *The Abolition of Man* (1943) by 'a few years' (Hooper).
7 'Consolation'—about 1945.
8 '*De Futilitate*'—during World War 2.
9 'The Funeral of a Great Myth'—perhaps after 1945.
10 'Finchley Avenue'—about 1950.
11 'The Psalms'—presumably before *Reflections on the Psalms* (1958), probably shortly before.
12 '*De Audiendis Poetis*' (first chapter of proposed book)—'several years before his retirement' (1963; Hooper).
13 'Forms of Things Unknown'—'towards the end of his life'.
14 'On Criticism'—'fairly late in the author's life' (Hooper).
15 'Spenser's Cruel Cupid'—'a few months before his death' (Hooper).
16 'The Genesis of a Medieval Book' (first chapter of proposed book)—'one of the last pieces he wrote' (Hooper).

1905	**1906**	**1907**	**1908**
17 (Boxen)	19 (Boxen)	21 Boxen	23 Boxen
18 Letter	20 Letter (?1906)	22 Letters	24 Letters

1909	**1910**	**1911**
25 Boxen	28 Boxen	30 (Boxen)
26 Letters	29 Letter	31 Letters
27 Diary		

A chronological list of the works of C. S. Lewis

1912
32 'The Expedition to Holly Bush Hill', *Cherbourg School Magazine*, November
33 Boxen
34 Letter

1913
35 'The Expedition to Holly Bush Hill', *Cherbourg School Magazine*, July (a different expedition!)
36 *'Quam Bene Saturno'*, *Cherbourg School Magazine*, July
37 'Are Athletes Better than Scholars?', *Cherbourg School Magazine*
38 Letters

1914
39 Letters

1915
40 'The Hills of Down', Easter
41 'Against Potpourri', Summer
42 'A Prelude', Summer
43 'Ballade of a Winter's Morning', Christmas
44 Letters

1916
45 *'Laus Mortis'*, Easter
46 'Sonnet—To Sir Philip Sydney', Autumn
47 'Of Ships', Christmas
48 'Couplets', Christmas
49 Letters

1917
50 'Circe—a Fragment', April
51 'Exercise', April
52 Letters

1918
53 Letters

Appendix 2

1919
54 'Death in Battle', *Reveille*, February (also in 55)
55 *Spirits in Bondage*, 20 March
56 Letters

1920
57 Letters

1921
58 Letters

1922
59 Diary (lengthy extracts from his diary of 1922–27 were published as *All My Road Before Me*)
60 Letters

1923
61 Diary
62 Letters

1924
63 'Joy', *The Beacon*, May
64 Diary
65 Letters

1925
66 Diary
67 Letters

1926
68 *Dymer*, 18 September
69 Diary
70 Letters

1927
71 Diary
72 Letters

1928
73 Review of *Rossetti: His Life and Works* by Evelyn Waugh, *The Oxford Magazine*, 25 October
74 Review of *Matthew Arnold* by Hugh Kingsmill, *The Oxford Magazine*, 15 November
75 Review of *Form and Style in Poetry* by W.P. Ker, *The Oxford Magazine*, 6 December
76 Letters

1929
77 Letter to *The Times Literary Supplement*, 18 April
78 Review of *Collins* by H.W. Garrod, *The Oxford Magazine*, 16 May
79 Letters

1930
80 Commentary on 'The Lay of Leithian', a narrative poem composed by his friend J.R.R. Tolkien, probably early 1930

81 'The Nameless Isle', August

82 'Leaving for Ever the Home of One's Youth'

83 Letters

1931

84 Letter to *The Review of English Studies*, January

85 Letters

1932

86 'A Note on *Comus*', *The Review of English Studies*, April

87 'What Chaucer Really Did to *Il Filostrato*', *Essays and Studies* (journal)

88 Letters

1933

89 *The Pilgrim's Regress*, 25 May

90 'Abecedarium Philosophicum' (with Owen Barfield), *The Oxford Magazine*, 30 November

91 Letters

1934

92 'Man is a Lumpe Where All Beasts Kneaded Be', *The Oxford Magazine*, 10 May

93 'Scholar's Melancholy', *The Oxford Magazine*, 24 May

94 Review of *The Three Estates in Medieval and Renaissance Literature* by Ruth Mohl, *Medium Ævum*, February

95 Review of *Sir Thomas Wyatt and Some Collected Studies* by E.K. Chambers, *Medium Ævum*, October

96 Review of *Longinus and English Criticism* by T.R. Henn, *The Oxford* Magazine, 6 December

97 'The Personal Heresy in Criticism', *Essays and Studies*

98 Letters

1935

99 'The Planets', *Lysistrata*, May

100 'The Alliterative Metre', *Lysistrata*, May

101 Letter to *The Times Literary Supplement*, 2 May

102 Letter to *The Times Literary Supplement,* 23 May

103 Letters

Appendix 2

1936

104 'Genius and Genius', *The Review of English Studies*, April

105 'Sonnet', *The Oxford Magazine*, 14 May

106 *The Allegory of Love: A Study in Medieval Tradition*, 21 May

107 'Open Letter to Dr Tillyard', *Essays and Studies*

108 Letters

1937

109 'Coronation March', *The Oxford Magazine*, 6 May

110 'After Kirby's *Kalevala*' (translation), *The Oxford Magazine*, 13 May

111 Review of *The Works of Morris and Yeats in Relation to Early Saga Literature* by Dorothy M. Hoare, *The Times Literary Supplement*, 29 May

112 Review of *The Hobbit* by J.R.R. Tolkien, *The Times Literary Supplement*, 2 October

113 Letters

1938

114 'The Future of Forestry', *The Oxford Magazine*, 10 February

115 'What the Bird Said Early in the Year', *The Oxford Magazine*, 19 May

116 'From Johnson's *Life of Fox*', *The Oxford Magazine*, 9 June

117 *Out of the Silent Planet*, 23 September

118 Letter to *The Times*, 18 November

119 'Pattern', *The Spectator*, 9 December

120 'The Fifteenth-Century Heroic Line', *Essays and Studies*

121 'Donne and Love Poetry in the Seventeenth Century', *Seventeenth-Century Studies Presented to Sir Herbert Grierson*

122 Letters

1939

123 *Rehabilitations and Other Essays*, 23 March (a book of nine essays of which it seems that only one had been published previously)

124 Review of *Taliessin through Logres* by Charles Williams, *Theology*, April

125 *The Personal Heresy: A Controversy* (with E.M.W. Tillyard), 27 April

126 Letter to *Theology*, May

127 'To the Author of *Flowering Rifle*', *The Cherwell*, 6 May

128 'Learning in War-Time', preached at St Mary's, Oxford, printed as pamphlet 22 October

129 Review of *A Lectionary of Christian Prose from the Second Century to the Twentieth Century*, A.C. Bouquet, ed., *Theology*, December

130 Letters

1940

131 'Dante's Similes', delivered at the Oxford Dante Society, 13 February

132 'Dangers of National Repentance', *The Guardian*, 15 March

133 'Two Ways with the Self', *The Guardian*, 3 May

134 Review of *Passion and Society* by D. de Rougemont and *The Bride of Christ* by Claude Chavasse, *Theology*, June

135 'The Necessity of Chivalry', *Time and Tide*, 17 August

136 *The Problem of Pain*, 18 October

137 Letter to *Theology*, November

138 'Christianity and Culture' (three parts), *Theology*, March, June, December

139 'Essence', part of 'A Pageant Played in Vain', 'Poem for Psychoanalysts and/or Theologians', and 'After Prayers, Lie Cold', *Fear No More: A Book of Poems for the Present Time by Living English Poets*

140 'Hermione in the House of Paulina', *Augury: An Oxford Miscellany of Verse and Prose*, Alex M. Hardie and Keith C. Douglas, eds

141 'Why I am Not a Pacifist', delivered at a pacifist society in Oxford

142 Letters

1941

143 Review of *The Oxford Book of Christian Verse*, Lord David Cecil, ed., *The Review of English Studies*, January

144 'Meditation on the Third Commandment', *The Guardian*, 10 January

145 Review of *Boethius: some aspects of his times and work* by Helen M. Barrett, *Medium Ævum*, February

146 'Evil and God', *The Spectator*, 7 February

147 Review of *Milton and His Modern Critics* by Logan Pearsall Smith, *The Cambridge Review*, 21 February

148 'Bulverism', *Time and Tide*, 29 March

149 'Religion: Reality or Substitute?', *World Dominion*, September-October, a few additions made 'a few years later' (Hooper)

150 Review of *The Mind of the Maker* by Dorothy L. Sayers, *Theology*, October

1944

178 Review of *English Literary Criticism: The Medieval Phase* by J.W.H. Atkins, *The Oxford Magazine*, 10 February

179 'Is English Doomed?', *The Spectator*, 11 February

180 'On the Reading of Old Books', Preface to *The Incarnation of the Word of God* by Athanasius; not long before 19 February

181 Letter to *The Listener*, 9 March

182 'The Parthenon and the Optative', *Time and Tide*, 11 March

183 'What France Means to You', *La France Libre*, 15 April. Seven contributors wrote on this subject in French, including Lewis.

184 *Answers to Questions on Christianity*, a transcript of a question session held 18 April, published as a pamphlet by the Electrical and Musical Industries Christian Fellowship

185 'Democratic Education', *Time and Tide*, 29 April

186 'A Dream', *The Spectator*, 28 July

187 'Myth Became Fact', *World Dominion*, September-October

188 'Blimpophobia', *Time and Tide*, 9 September

189 'The Death of Words', *The Spectator*, 22 September

190 'Horrid Red Things', *Church of England Newspaper*, 6 October

191 *Beyond Personality*, 9 October; some chapters previously published in *The Listener*, 24 February-6 April.

192 Letter to *The Times Literary Supplement*, 2 December.

193 'Private Bates', *The Spectator*, 29 December

194 'Christian Reunion' (probably 1944)

195 'The Inner Ring' at King's College, London

196 Letters

1945

197 'Religion and Science', *The Coventry Evening Telegraph*, 3 January

198 Letter to *The Times Literary Supplement*, 3 February

199 Letter to *The Times Literary Supplement*, 10 February

200 'Two Lectures', *The Coventry Evening Telegraph*, 21 February

201 Review of *Romanticism Comes of Age* by Owen Barfield, *The Spectator*, 9 March

202 'Christian Apologetics', delivered at the Camarthen Conference for Youth Leaders and Junior Clergy (Anglican) at Easter (Easter Sunday was 29 March)

203 'The Laws of Nature', *The Coventry Evening Telegraph*, 4 April

204 'The Grand Miracle', *The Guardian*, 27 April

205 'Charles Walter Stansby Williams' (obituary), *The Oxford Magazine*, 24 May

206 'Work and Prayer', *The Coventry Evening Telegraph*, 28 May

207 'Membership', *Sobornost*, June

208 'The Salamander', *The Spectator*, 8 June

209 'Hedonics', *Time and Tide*, 16 June

210 'Oliver Elton (1861–1945)' (obituary), *The Oxford Magazine*, 21 June

211 Letter to *The Times Literary Supplement*, 14 July

212 'Meditation in a Toolshed', *The Coventry Evening Telegraph*, 17 July

213 'To Charles Williams', *Britain To-day*, August

214 *That Hideous Strength*, 16 August

215 Letter to *The Guardian*, 31 August

216 'The Condemned', *The Spectator*, 7 September

217 'The Sermon and the Lunch', *Church of England Newspaper*, 21 September

218 'Scraps', *St James Magazine*, December (of St James, Birkdale, Southport)

219 'After Priggery—What?', *The Spectator*, 7 December

220 'On the Atomic Bomb', *The Spectator*, 28 December

221 Epitaph no.12 (in *Poems*), *Time and Tide*, 29 December

222 'Is Theology Poetry?', *The Socratic Digest*

223 Recollection of George Gordon's 'Discussion Class', *The Life of George S. Gordon 1881–1942* by M.C.G.

224 'Addison', *Essays on the Eighteenth Century Presented to David Nichol Smith*

225 'From the Latin of Milton's *De Idea Platonica Quemadmodum Aristoteles Intellexit*' (translation) in *English*

226 Letters

1946

227 'The Birth of Language', *Punch*, 9 January

228 *The Great Divorce*, 14 January (previously published in *The Guardian* 10 November 1944–13 April 1945)

229 *George MacDonald: an Anthology*, 18 March; Lewis selected and arranged the extracts and wrote a preface.

230 'On Being Human', *Punch*, 8 May

231 'Miserable Offenders', *Five Sermons by Laymen* (St Matthew's, Northampton, April-May)

232 'Different Tastes in Literature', *Time and Tide*, 25 May and 1 June

233 Letter to *The Oxford Magazine*, 13 June

234 Letter to *The Sunday Times*, 11 August

235 'Solomon', *Punch*, 14 August

236 'Religion without Dogma?', *The Phoenix Quarterly*, Autumn; a slightly fuller form was printed in *The Socratic Digest* No.4 (1948)

237 'A Reply to Professor Haldane' (unfinished; Haldane's article appeared Autumn)

238 'Talking about Bicycles', *Resistance*, October

239 'The True Nature of Gnomes', *Punch*, 16 October

240 'Period Criticism', *Time and Tide*, 9 November

241 'The Decline of Religion', *The Cherwell*, 29 November

242 'The Meteorite', *Time and Tide*, 7 December (also in *Miracles* [1947])

243 'Man or Rabbit?', a pamphlet probably 1946

244 'Modern Man and his Categories of Thought'

245 'On the Transmission of Christianity', Preface to *How Heathen is Britain?* by G.B. Sandhurst

246 Letters

1947

247 'Pan's Purge', *Punch*, 15 January

248 'The Prudent Jailer' *New English Weekly*, 16 January

249 Review of *'Paradise Lost' in Our Time: Some Comments* by Douglas Bush, *The Oxford Magazine*, 13 February

250 *Miracles*, 12 May

251 'Young King Cole', *Punch*, 21 May

252 'The *Morte Darthur*', *The Times Literary Supplement*, 7 June

253 Letter to *The Guardian*, 27 June

254 'Two Kinds of Memory', *Time and Tide*, 7 August

255 '*Le Roi S'Amuse*', *Punch*, 1 October

256 Letter to *Church Times*, 3 October

257 'Donkey's Delight', *Punch*, 5 November

258 Letter to *The Times Literary Supplement*, 29 November

259 'The Last of the Wine', *Punch*, 3 December

260 *Essays Presented to Charles Williams*, 4 December; Lewis edited this, contributing the Preface and the essay 'On Stories'.

261 'On Forgiveness', in the parish magazine of St Mary's, Sawston, Cambridgeshire

262 'Vivisection' (pamphlet, New England Anti-Vivisection Society)

Appendix 2

289 'On Church Music', *English Church Music*, April

290 'On a Picture by Chirico', *The Spectator*, 6 May

291 'The Adam at Night', *Punch*, 11 May

292 Letter to *Church Times*, 20 May

293 Epitaph no.17 (in *Poems*), *The Month*, July

294 Letter to *Church Times*, 1 July

295 Letter to *Church Times*, 15 July

296 'The Magician and the Dryad', *Punch*, 20 July

297 Letter to *Church Times*, 5 August

298 'The Day with a White Mark', *Punch*, 17 August

299 'The Adam Unparadised', *Punch*, 14 September

300 'The Humanitarian Theory of Punishment', *20th Century: An Australian Quarterly Review*

301 *Transposition and Other Addresses*, containing five items, all of which except 'Transposition' had been previously published

302 'Pindar Sang', *Mandrake*

303 Letters

1950

304 'The Pains of Animals', *The Month*, February

305 Letter to *The Times Literary Supplement*, 3 March

306 'As One Oldster to Another', *Punch*, 15 March

307 'The Literary Impact of the Authorised Version', delivered at the University of London, 20 March, published some time same year

308 Review of *This Ever Diverse Pair,* G.A.L. Burgeon (Owen Barfield), *Time and Tide*, 25 March

309 'A Cliché Came Out of its Cage', *Nine: A Magazine of Poetry and Criticism*, May

310 'Historicism', *The Month*, October

311 *The Lion, the Witch and the Wardrobe*, 16 October

312 'What are we to make of Jesus Christ?', *Asking Them Questions*, Third Series, Ronald Selby Wright, ed.

313 Letters

1951

314 'Ballade of Dead Gentlemen', *Punch*, 23 March

315 Letter to *Essays in Criticism*, July

316 Letter to *Church Times*, 10 August

341 *'Odora Canum Vis'*, *The Month*, May

342 'Science-Fiction Cradlesong', *The Times Literary Supplement*, 11 June

343 'On Punishment: A Reply' (to answers to his 'Humanitarian Theory of Punishment', 1949), *Res Judicatae*, August

344 'Tolkien's *Lord of the Rings*', Part 1 (a review of volume 1), *Time and Tide*, 14 August

345 *The Horse and His Boy*, 6 September

346 *English Literature in the Sixteenth Century, Excluding Drama* (a volume in the Oxford History of English Literature), 16 September

347 *'De Descriptione Temporum'*, inaugural lecture at Cambridge, delivered 29 November, published shortly afterwards

348 'A Confession', *Punch*, 1 December

349 'Xmas and Christmas', *Time and Tide*, 4 December

350 'Edmund Spenser, 1552–99', *Major British Writers* (vol.1)

351 'A Note on Jane Austen', *Essays in Criticism*

352 Reminiscence in *Paul Victor Mendelssohn Benecke 1868–1944,* Margaret Deneke, ed.

353 Letters

1955

354 'George Orwell', *Time and Tide*, 8 January

355 'On a Theme from Nicholas of Cusa', *The Times Literary Supplement*, 21 January

356 'Prudery and Philology', *The Spectator*, 21 January

357 'Legion', *The Month*, April

358 'Lilies that Fester', *Twentieth Century*, April

359 *The Magician's Nephew*, 2 May

360 Letter to *The Times* (with Dorothy L. Sayers), 14 May

361 'On Obstinacy in Belief', both *The Sewanee Review*, Autumn, and *The Socratic Digest*

362 Letter to *The Listener*, 15 September

363 *Surprised by Joy*, 19 September

364 'Tolkien's *Lord of the Rings*', Part 2 (a review of volumes 2 and 3), *Time and Tide*, 22 October

365 'On Science Fiction', delivered at the Cambridge University English Club, 24 November

366 Foreword to *Smoke on the Mountain* by Joy Davidman

367 Letters

1956

368 'The Shoddy Lands', *Magazine of Fantasy and Science Fiction*, February

395 'On Juvenile Tastes' in *Church Times, Children's Book Supplement*, 28 November

396 Letter to *The Times Literary Supplement*, 28 November

397 Letter to *The Christian Century*, 31 December

398 'A Tribute to E. R. Eddison', printed on the dust jacket of Eddison's posthumous *The Mezentian Gate*

399 Letters

1959

400 'The Efficacy of Prayer', *The Atlantic Monthly*, January

401 'Fern-seed and Elephants', delivered at Westcott House, Cambridge, 11 May

402 'An Expostulation', *Magazine of Fantasy and Science Fiction*, June

403 '*Molliter Ossa Cubent*' (obituary of Jane McNeill), *The Campbellian* (magazine of Campbell College, Belfast), July

404 'Screwtape Proposes a Toast', *The Saturday Evening Post*, 19 December

405 'Good Work and Good Works', *Good Work*, Christmas

406 *After Ten Years* (unfinished), chapters 1–4

407 Letters

1960

408 Letter to *The Times Literary Supplement*, 1 January

409 'Metre', *A Review of English Literature*, January

410 Letter to *Delta: The Cambridge Literary Magazine*, February

411 Review of *Arthurian Literature in the Middle Ages*, R.S.Loomis, ed., *The Cambridge Review*, 13 February

412 'The Language of Religion', was to have been delivered March; Lewis was ill.

413 'Undergraduate Criticism', *Broadsheet* (Cambridge University), 9 March

414 *The Four Loves*, 28 March

415 Review of *The Allegory of the 'Faerie Queen'* by M. Pauline Parker, *The Cambridge Review*, 11 June

416 Review of *Shakespeare and the Rose of Love* by John Vyvyan, *The Listener*, 7 July

417 'It all began with a picture...', *Radio Times*, 15 July

418 'The Mythopoeic Gift of Rider Haggard', *Time and Tide*, 3 September

419 *Studies in Words*, 9 September

420 Preface to *A Faith of Our Own* by Austin Farrer

421 *After Ten Years* (unfinished; a further passage)

422 New edition of *Miracles* (slightly revised)

423 Letters

1961

424 *The Screwtape Letters and Screwtape Proposes a Toast* (published together, with a new preface), 27 February

425 A review of *Neoplatonism in the Poetry of Spenser* by Robert Ellrodt, *Études Anglaises*, April-June

426 'Four-Letter Words', *The Critical Quarterly*, Summer

427 *A Grief Observed*, 29 September

428 'Before We Can Communicate', *Breakthrough*, October

429 *An Experiment in Criticism*, 13 October

430 Letter to *Church Times*, 1 December

431 Letter to *Church Times*, 15 December

432 Letters

1962

433 Review of *The Death of Tragedy* by George Steiner, *Encounter*, February

434 *They Asked for a Paper*, 26 February (twelve papers, all, I think, previously published with the exception of 'A Slip of the Tongue')

435 Review of *The Erotic in Literature* by David Loth, *The Observer*, 4 March

436 Review of *The Life of Samuel Johnson* by Sir John Hawkins, B. H. Davis, ed., *The Sunday Telegraph*, 1 April

437 Letter to *English*, Summer

438 Letter to *Church Times*, 20 July

439 Review of Robert Fitzgerald's translation of Homer's *Odyssey*, *The Sunday Telegraph*, 9 September

440 'Sex in Literature', *The Sunday Telegraph*, 30 September

441 'Going into Europe: A Symposium' in *Encounter*, December

442 'Unreal Estates', a conversation recorded 4 December, not published till after his death

443 'The Vision of John Bunyan', *The Listener*, 13 December

444 Review of *On Aristotle and Greek Tragedy* by John Jones, *The Sunday Telegraph*, 16 December

445 'The Anthropological Approach', *English and Medieval Studies Presented to J.R.R. Tolkien on the Occasion of his Seventieth Birthday,* Norman Davis and C.L. Wrenn, eds

446 Letters

1963

447 Letter to *Encounter*, January

448 'The Seeing Eye', *Show*, February

449 'Must Our Image of God Go?', *The Observer*, 24 March

450 Review of *The Visionary Company: A Reading of English Romantic Poetry* by Harold Bloom, *Encounter*, June

451 'Epitaph for Helen Joy Davidman' on marble at the Oxford Crematorium, July

452 'Cross-Examination' (transcript of interview) in *Decision*, September/October

453 Review of *The Poetry of Search and the Poetry of Statement* by Dorothy L. Sayers, *The Sunday Telegraph*, 1 December

454 'We Have No "Right to Happiness"', *The Saturday Evening Post*, 21–28 December

455 Introduction to *Selections from Layamon's 'Brut'*, G. L. Brooks, ed.

456 'The English Prose "Morte"', *Essays on Malory*, J. A. W. Bennett, ed.

457 Letters

1964

458 *Letters to Malcolm: Chiefly on Prayer*, 27 January

459 *The Discarded Image: An Introduction to Medieval and Renaissance Literature*, 7 May

460 *Poems*, 26 October

3 A Scripture index to the works of C. S. Lewis

C. S. Lewis often quoted Scripture, or used a scriptural expression, without giving a reference. The aim of this index is to provide a catalogue of his use of Scripture. Occasionally, I have missed out some use of Scripture from Lewis's writings because it did not seem to shed any light on his view and use of Scripture—for example, it may have been a merely humorous use of a scriptural phrase. I may also have mistakenly included references that do not shed any such light, or overlooked some that do.

Overall, of course the entries are placed in biblical order. However, within the sections of general references (references to the Bible in general, the Old Testament in general, and so on), they are placed in chronological order—the order in which the works in question appear in Appendix 2. This is also the case where there is more than one reference to a particular verse or passage.

Some of the references in Lewis's works, particularly those given in the sections on the Gospels, are not direct quotations but simply a reference to a particular event, such as the sign at Cana or the feeding of the five thousand. Where the event in question is recorded in more than one Bible book, references to each relevant book are included. In the same way, an expression found in more than one place in the Bible is given more than one reference; although those that occur many times have not been included at all. In the case of events recorded in more than one Bible book, and concerning which Lewis does not mention any particular book but uses an expression which does not occur in all, only the source(s) of the expression are referenced.

Lewis's fictional and pre-conversion works are not included.

Abbreviations and editions

For the purposes of this index it is inconvenient that most, if not all, of Lewis's works are available in more than one edition. The following list gives details of the editions that have been used in compiling the index. The date given is the date of the first publication *of that edition*, and if it is a reprint and the date of the reprint is known, that date is added. The number of pages is also given. In these ways it is hoped that users will be able to discover quickly whether their own editions correspond. The works are listed in alphabetical order of the abbreviations employed.

After this there is a second list, giving details of those of Lewis's works which are quoted in this book but do not appear in the first list.

AGO   *A Grief Observed* (Faber and Faber, 1966). Paperback, 64pp.

AM   *The Abolition of Man* (Fount, 1999). Paperback, 69pp.

Chr.Ref.   *Christian Reflections* (Walter Hooper, ed.) (Fount, 1981 (repr.1991)). Paperback, 219pp.

Chr.Reunion   *Christian Reunion and Other Essays* (Walter Hooper, ed.), Fount Paperback, 113pp.

CLII   *Collected Letters Volume II: Books, Broadcasts and War 1931–1949* (Walter Hooper, ed.) (HarperCollins, 2004). Hardback, 1132pp.

Dis.Im.   *The Discarded Image: An Introduction to Medieval and Renaissance Literature* (Cambridge University Press, 1994 (repr. 1995)). Paperback, 232pp.

Dock   *God in the Dock: Essays on Theology* (Walter Hooper, ed.) (Fount, 1979). Paperback, 108pp.

EC   *Essay Collection and Other Short Pieces* (Lesley Walmsley, ed.), HarperCollins 2000. Hardback, 894pp.

E.Lit.16C   *English Literature in the Sixteenth Century Excluding Drama*, (Oxford University Press, 1973). Paperback, 567pp.

FL   *The Four Loves* (Fount, 1977). Paperback, 128pp.

FSE   *Fern-seed and Elephants and other essays on Christianity* (Walter Hooper, ed.) (Fount, 1977). Paperback, 125pp.

FST   *First and Second Things: Essays on Theology and Ethics* (Walter Hooper, ed.) (Fount, 1985). Paperback, 128pp.

GMAnth.   *George MacDonald: An Anthology* (ed. with Preface by C. S. Lewis) (Fount, 1983 (repr. 1990)). Paperback, 187pp.

LM   *Letters to Malcolm: Chiefly on Prayer*, Geoffrey Bles 1964. Hardback, 159pp.

M   *Miracles: A Preliminary Study*, Fount 1974. Paperback, 190pp.

Appendix 3

MC	*Mere Christianity*, Fontana 1955 (repr.1962). Paperback, 188pp.
PC	*Present Concerns: Ethical Essays* (Walter Hooper, ed.) (Fount, 1986 (repr. 1991)). Paperback, 108pp.
Poems	*The Collected Poems of C. S. Lewis* (Walter Hooper, ed.) (Fount 1994). Paperback, 263pp.
PP	*The Problem of Pain* (Fount, 1977 (repr. 1990)). Paperback, 125pp.
PPL	*A Preface to Paradise Lost* (Oxford University Press, 1960 (repr. 1975)). Paperback, 143pp.
Pref.Smoke	Preface to *Smoke on the Mountain* by Joy Davidman (Hodder and Stoughton, 1953 (repr. 1955)). Preface on pp. 7–11.
RP	*Reflections on the Psalms* (Fount, 1977). Paperback, 128pp.
SBJ	*Surprised by Joy: The shape of my early life* (Fount, 1977). Paperback, 190pp.
SW	*Studies in Words* (Cambridge University Press, 1990 (repr. 2000)) Paperback, 343pp.
Toast	*Screwtape Proposes a Toast and other pieces* (Fount, 1977). Paperback, 126pp.
WL	*Letters of C. S. Lewis edited, with a Memoir by W. H. Lewis* (Walter Hooper, ed.) (Fount, 1988). Paperback, 528pp.

* * *

Collected Letters Volume I: Family Letters 1905–1931, (HarperCollins, 2000).
Perelandra (Scribner 1996).
The Magician's Nephew (Penguin, 1968).
The Lion, the Witch and the Wardrobe (Penguin, 1968).
The Horse and his Boy (Penguin, 1968).
Prince Caspian (Penguin, 1968).
The Voyage of the Dawn Treader (Penguin, 1967).
The Silver Chair (Penguin, 1966).
The Last Battle (Penguin, 1968).

WL 410

E.Lit.16C 500

SBJ 160

RP 9–14

FL 103

1:1 **RP** 64

1:2 **RP** 50

2 **CLII** 383, **RP** 101

2:4 **RP** 11

3:2 **Chr.Ref.** 162

5:10 **RP** 65

6:5 **RP** 37

7:3–5 **RP** 21–2

8 **RP** 110–2

8:6 **RP** 111

9:2 **RP** 47

9:8–9 **Chr.Ref.**158

9:8, 12 **RP** 17

10:2 **RP** 20

10:7 **RP** 65

10:14 **Chr.Ref.**162

11:3 **Chr.Ref.** 162

11:7 **Chr.Ref.** 44, 106

11:8 **PP**19, **RP** 54

12:3 **RP** 65

12:9 **Chr.Ref.** 162

13 **RP** 101

14:1 **Chr.Ref.** 162

16:11 **RP** 99

17:1 **Chr.Ref.**159

17:3 **RP** 112

17:13–14 **RP** 34–5

18 **Chr.Ref.** 147, **RP** 10, 52

18:10 **RP** 70

18:11 **RP** 70

19 **Pref.Smoke** 8–9, **RP** 56–7, 70

19:8–9 **RP** 49

19:10 **EC** 164, **RP** 49–57

22 **RP** 99, 101

22:3, 17 **RP** 106

22:6 **Chr.Ref.** 163

22:7 **Chr.Ref.** 162

22:8 **Chr.Ref.** 162

23 **RP** 24

24 **CLII** 884

26:1 **Chr.Ref.** 159, **RP** 112

26:4–5 **RP** 58

27:4 **RP** 42–8, 79

29:3–5 **RP** 70

29:9 **M** 118

30:3 **RP** 37

30:10 **RP** 37, 78

31:7 **RP** 58

31:13 **Chr.Ref.** 162

31:20 **RP** 65

33:4, 9 **RP** 71

34:8 **M** 94, **RP** 75

35:1 **Chr.Ref.** 159

35:11 **PPL** 82

35:12–14 **RP** 21

35:23 **RP** 16

35:24 **RP** 15

36:1, 5 **RP** 113

36:3 **RP** 65

36:5–6 **RP** 70

36:6 **CLII** 815, **RP** 54

36:9 **Dock** 34

37:1 **CLII** 746

37:6 **RP** 11

38:11 **Chr.Ref.** 162

38:13 **Chr.Ref.** 163

38:16 **Chr.Ref.** 163

39:1 **CLII** 76

39:6 **RP** 37

40:8, 9, 15 **RP** 106–7

41:7 **RP** 65

42 **RP** 47

42:1 **RP** 39

42:2 **EC** 164

42:3 **Chr.Ref.** 162

43:1 **Chr.Ref.** 159

43:4 **RP** 47

44:15 **Chr.Ref.** 162

45 **RP** 107–110

45:4–6 **RP** 104

45:11 **RP** 109

46:1 **AGO** 8

47:1 **RP** 48

49:7–8 **RP** 35

49:8 **RP** 48

49:10 **RP** 37

49:19 **RP** 37

50:2 **RP** 47

50:6–21 **RP** 21

50:10, 12 **Chr.Ref.** 129

50:12 **RP** 46, 79

50:18 **RP** 58

50:21 **RP** 83

50:23 **RP** 77

52:3 **RP** 65

54:1, 6 **RP** 78

55 **RP** 101

55:22 **RP** 65

57:9 **RP** 47

Appendix 3

7:6 **WL** 501

7:7 **RP** 12, **AGO** 40, **LM** 81

7:9 **LM** 75

7:11 **Dock** 80

7:12 **AM** 25, 54, **MC** 74–5, 78

7:13–14 **CLII** 450, **Poems** 143

7:13 **SW** 242

7:14 **CLII** 283, 1008

7:15 **CLII** 868

7:16–20 **MC** 172

7:16 **MC** 165

7:20 **CLII** 23

7:22 **MC** 109

8:5–13 **EC** 291

8:13 **Chr.Ref.** 183

8:23–27 **M** 145

9:6 **CLII** 502

9:8 **FL** 13

9:10–13 **RP** 60

9:12 **WL** 460, **FSE** 89, **Chr.Ref.** 218, **Dock** 80

9:22 **Chr.Ref.** 183

9:28 **Chr.Ref.** 184

10:16 **CLII** 142, **M** 168, **Chr.Ref.** 128, **MC** 70, 119, **SW** 171–2

10:23 **PP** 88

10:28 **PP** 99

10:29 **CLII** 511, **M** 178, **LM** 78

10:31 **FST** 80

10:39 **CLII** 13, **PP** 81, 119, **CLII** 617, **M**129, **Dock** 84,

MC188

11:6 **AGO** 56

11:28–30 **Dock** 84

11:28 **FL** 9

11:29 **FSE** 111

11:30 **CLII** 189, **MC**164

11:39 **Chr.Ref.** 180–90

12:32 **SW** 228, 234

12:33–5 **MC** 172

12:36 **Poems** 149

12:39 **Dock** 25

12:44 **CLII** 328

12:48 **Chr.Ref.** 30

13:5, 20 **RP** 74–5

13:12 **AGO** 40

13:22 **SW** 225, 238

13:45–6 **PP**118

14:15–21 **Dock** 17, **M**140

14:22–33 **M** 145

14:26 **Dock** 12, 21

14:29 **Dock** 65

14:31 **Chr.Ref.** 184

15:2 **Chr.Ref.** 55

15:21–28 **WL** 448–9

15:28 **Chr.Ref.** 183

15:32–37 **M** 140

16:4 **Dock** 25

16:16–17 **Chr.Ref.** 214–5

16:19 **SW** 236

16:23 **FL** 113

16:24 **M** 82, **MC** 164

16:25 **CLII**1?, **PP** 81, 119, **CLII** 617, **M** 129, **Dock** 84, **MC**188

16:26 **SW** 257

17:1–8 **Dock** 20, **M**146, 156–7

17:5 **PP** 39, **M** 160, **MC**168

17:12–13 **CLII** 431–2

17:20 **M** 139, **Chr.Ref.** 189, **LM** 83

17:25 **WL** 460

18:3 **Chr.Ref.** 30, **CLII**999

18:3–4 **CLII** 93

18:4 **CLII** 480

18:7 **PP** 88–9

18:8–9 **FSE** 23, **Dock** 84

18:8 **RP** 32

18:9 **FSE** 32, 34, **WL** 408, **FL** 27

18:11–14 **EC** 156

18:12–13 **CLII** 556, **Chr.Ref.** 218

18:12 **Dock** 33, **FSE** 89

18:19 **Chr.Ref.** 186

18:23–35 **CLII** 410

19:5–6 **CLII** 394, 512, **MC** 92

19:12 **Chr.Ref.** 29, **CLII** 381

19:16–17 **PP**36

19:18 **WL** 429

19:23–4 **MC** 177–8, **FL** 10, 124

19:24 **CLII** 527, **Poems** 143

19:24–6 **Poems** 148

19:26 **PP** 21, 23

19:30 **Dock** 84, **MC** 179

20:16 **Dock** 84, **MC** 179

21:18–22 **M** 144–5

21:19 **Dock** 17

21:21–2 **Chr.Ref.** 184–5

21:21 **M** 139, **Chr.Ref.** 189, **LM** 83

21:22 **CLII** 361, 367

21:23–27 **CLII** 192

21:31 **WL** 437

22:13 **PP** 99

22:15–22 **CLII** 192, **FSE** 31

22:23–33 **CLII** 192

22:30 **Toast** 88

22:34–40 **CLII** 118, 616

22:35–40 **M** 160

22:36–40 **LM** 45

22:37 **MC** 115

22:39–40 **FL** 27

22:39 **CLII** 408, **MC** 101, **LM** 147

23:8 **Chr.Ref.** 30

23:9 **M** 143

23:23–4 **RP** 51–2

23:24 **Dock** 80

23:37 **PP** 38

24:6 **CLII** 843, 869, 979

24:14 **SW** 224

24:15 **CLII** 327

24:23 **FSE** 80

24:24 **Toast** 69, **FSE** 95

24:30 **FSE** 84

24:35 **EC** 149

24:42–4 **FSE** 79

25:1–13 **PP** 99

25:21, 23 **CLII** 480, **MC** 110

25:29 **AGO** 40

25:30–46 **WL** 432–3

25:31–46 **PP** 91, **CLII** 499, **MC** 77, **WL** 418, 428,

438, **RP** 15–16, **FL** 118, **LM** 98

25:34, 41 **PP** 100

25:46 **PP** 99, **SW** 228

26:26–8 **LM** 132

26:26 **Dock** 60, 26

26:36–27:46 **LM** 62–5

26:36–46 **FSE** 98

26:36–44 **CLII** 266–8, **PP** 88, **LM** 53

26:39–44 **CLII** 765, 814

26:39 **CLII** 764, 842

26:63–4 **Dock** 80

26:64 **CLII** 916, **FSE** 65

26:72, 74 **RP** 63

27:5 **WL** 480

27:26 **EC** 154

27:34 **Chr.Ref.** 190

27:42 **CLII** 953, **Chr.Ref.** 190

27:46 **PP** 82, **FSE** 103, **AGO** 8.

MARK
GENERAL

M 138

1:15 **SW** 236

2:10–11 **CLII** 502

2:15–17 **RP** 60

2:17 **FSE** 89, **Chr.Ref.** 218

2:19 **Dock** 80

4:5, 16–17 **RP** 74–5

4:11 **SW** 236

4:21 **LM** 131

4:25 **AGO** 40

4:35–41 **M** 145

5:9 **CLII** 816, **SBJ** 181

6:5 **CLII** 814

6:35–44 **Dock** 17, **M** 140

6:45–52 **M** 145

6:50 **Dock** 12, 21

7:2 **Chr.Ref.** 55

7:24–30 **WL** 448–9

8:1–9 **M** 140

8:11–12 **Dock** 25

8:27–38 **FSE** 108–9

8:33 **FL** 113

8:34 **M** 82, **MC** 164

8:35, 38 **Dock** 84

8:35 **CLII** 13, **PP** 81, 119, **CLII** 617, **M** 129, **MC** 188

9:2–8 **Dock** 20, **M** 146, 156–7

9:7 **M** 160

9:24 **WL** 419, **LM** 84

9:35 **Dock** 84

9:43–48 **FSE** 23, **Dock** 84

9:43–4 **RP** 32

9:47 **FSE** 32, 34, **WL** 408, **FL** 27

10:8 **CLII** 394, 512, **MC** 92

10:15 **CLII** 93, 480, 999

10:17–18 **PP** 36

10:19 **MC** 104, **WL** 429

10:23–4 **MC** 177–8, **FL** 10, 124

10:23 **CLII** 983

10:25–27 **Poems** 148

10:25 **CLII** 527, **Poems** 143

10:27 **PP** 21, 23, 83

10:30 **WL** 460

10:31 **Dock** 84, **MC** 179

11:12–14, 20–24 **M**144–5

11:14, 20 **Dock** 17

11:23–4 **Chr.Ref.** 186

11:23 **M** 139, **Chr.Ref.** 189, **LM** 83

11:24 **CLII** 361, 367, **FSE** 97–8, **LM** 80–1, 83

11:27–33 **CLII** 192

12:10 **RP** 99

12:13–17 **CLII** 192, **FSE** 31

12:18–27 **CLII** 192

12:25 **Toast** 88

12:28–31 **CLII** 118, 616, **M** 166, **LM** 45

12:30 **MC** 115

12:31 **CLII** 408, **MC** 101, **FL** 27, **LM** 147

12:35–7 **RP** 99, 101, 103

13:7 **CLII** 843, 869

13:14 **CLII** 327

13:21 **FSE** 80

13:22 **FSE** 95

13:30–32 **FSE** 69–70

13:31 **EC** 149

13:32–37 **FSE** 79–80

14:22–3 **LM** 132

14:22 **Dock** 26, 60

14:32–15:34 **LM** 62–5

14:32–42 **FSE** 98

14:32–41 **CLII** 814, **LM** 53

14:32–39 **CLII** 266–8, **PP** 88

14:36 **Chr.Ref.** 180–90

14:61–2 **Dock** 80

14:62 **CLII** 916, 1013

15:15 **EC** 154

15:23 **Chr.Ref.** 190

15:31 **CLII** 953, **Chr.Ref.** 90

15:34 **PP** 82, **FSE** 70, **RP** 99, **FSE** 103, **AGO** 8

16:6 **AM** 30

16:9–20 **M** 152

16:18 **FSE** 14–15

16:19 **M** 152, 159

LUKE

1–2 **CLII** 31, **WL** 411

1:1–4 **WL** 480

1:5–13 **CLII** 532

1:38 **Dock** 89

1:46–55 **Chr.Ref.** 148, 151, 154, 155, 157

1:46–54 **RP** 13

1:52 **CLII** 802

1:68 **Dock** 34

2:1 **SW** 224

2:29 **WL** 488

2:48 **WL** 463

3:12–14 **Chr.Ref.** 36

3:14 **CLII** 233, **EC** 290, 291, **MC** 104, **WL** 429

3:22 **PP** 39

3:23–38 **WL** 480

4:1–13 **CLII** 266–7, 522

4:3–4 **M** 180

4:3 **Dock** 17

4:20 **RP** 43

5:24 **CLII** 502

5:29–32 **RP** 60

5:31 **FSE** 89, **Chr.Ref.** 218

5:34 **Dock** 80

5:39 **WL** 506

6:20 **PP** 86, 88, **MC** 177–8

6:24 **RP** 34

6:26 **Chr.Ref.** 30

6:43–45 **MC** 172

6:46 **CLII** 605

7:1–10 **EC** 291

7:9 **WL** 429

7:23 **AGO** 56

7:36–50 **CLII** 192, **FL** 102–3

8:18 **AGO** 40

8:22–25 **M** 145

8:30 **CLII** 816

8:45 **FSE** 72

9:12–17 **Dock** 17, **M** 140

9:23 **M** 82, 166, **MC** 164

9:24, 26 **Dock** 84

9:24 **CLII** 13, **PP** 81, 119, **CLII** 617, **M** 129, **MC** 188

9:28–36 **M** 156–7

9:34 **M** 160

9:55 **WL** 501

10:19 **M** 139

10:30–35 **WL** 438

10:38–42 **CLII** 396

11:2–4 **PP** 36, **MC** 157

11:2 **CLII** 37, 361, 960, **Dock** 85, **LM** 27

11:3 **FSE** 37, 101, **FST** 41, **WL** 416, **Chr.Ref.** 180–1, **WL** 432

11:4 **CLII** 408, **MC** 101, **RP** 64

11:9 **AGO** 40, **LM** 81

5:19 **Chr.Ref.** 21, **Dock** 15, **M** 140

6:5–13 **M** 140

6:5–11 **Dock** 17

6:19 **Dock** 12, 21

6:44 **CLII** 915

6:48–58 **Dock** 84

6:53 **WL** 402

7:7 **SW** 233

7:17 **M** 94, **CLII** 816, 823, **WL** 419, **SBJ** 180–1

7:49 **AM** 29–30&n, **RP** 51

8:1–11 **RP** 160

8:3–8 **EC** 157

8:6, 8 **Dock** 82, **FSE** 108

8:48 **FL** 53

8:58 **CLII** 916, **Dock** 81

9:1–4 **WL** 418

9:4 **FL** 125

9:13 **FSE** 47

9:8–41 **FSE** 108

10:15 **Chr.Ref.** 20

10:16 **CLII** 70

10:34–5 **MC** 171, 184

11:5 **FL** 111

11:25 **M** 134, **Dock** 84

11:35 **Dock** 64, **M** 129, **CLII** 764, **FST** 94–5, **FL** 111

11:38–44 **M** 154–5

11:39 **M** 133

11:43–4 **WL** 487, **Poems** 139

11:49–52 **WL** 480

11:51 **AM** 68 NB misprinted as '13:51'

12:19 **SW** 230

12:24–5 **AM** 63

12:24 **PP** 119, **Dock** 60, **MC** 97, **LM** 42

12:48 **PP** 98

13:16 **LM** 54, 63

13:30 **FSE** 108

14:2 **PP** 117, **M** 153, 159, **LM** 155

14:6 **Dock** 84

14:9 **Dock** 85

14:12 **M** 139

14:13–14 **FSE** 97–8

14:13 **Chr.Ref.** 186

14:16–18 **CLII** 651, 656

15:1 **CLII** 916

15:9 **Chr.Ref.** 20

15:16 **FL** 83

15:20 **LM** 54, 63

16:7 **CLII** 651, 656, **RP** 106

16:33 **Dock** 84

17:1, 4, 5, **PP** 121

17:21 **CLII** 814

19:1 **EC** 154

19:25 **Dock** 89

20:14 **Dock** 23

20:15 **M** 151

20:29 **Toast** 73

20:30 **Dock** 25

21:4 **M** 151

21:18–19 **M** 8

21:22 **MC** 7

21:25 **WL** 460

ACTS

GENERAL

M 138, 147

WL 467

1:7 **CLII** 948

1:9 **M** 152

1:11 **FSE** 65

1:18–19 **WL** 480

1:22 **M** 147

2:27 **RP** 99

2:32 **M** 147

7:22 **RP** 74

7:57–60 **Poems** 139

8:27–38 **RP** 99, 101

9:1–9 **CLII** 189, **M** 148, **MC** 126

9:6 **WL** 412

10:2 **RP** 101

10:34 **FSE** 18 (AV imperfectly remembered), **CLII** 194

11:26 **MC** 11

13:15 **RP** 43

17:18 **M** 147

17:23 **M** 140

?17:26 **WL** 427

17:27 **RP** 75

17:30 **RP** 69

20:35 **CLII** 927, 935, **FL** 121

21:9 **Dock** 89

23:1 **SW** 192

24:1–8 **LM** 68–9

24:16 **SW** 192

Appendix 3

PAUL—GENERAL
CLII 194
EC 426
PP 53, 69, 111
CLII 326
FSE 15
CLII 881
CLII 914, 940, 989
WL 432–3
E.Lit.16C 385
SBJ 54
WL 448
RP 95–6
LM 90

ROMANS
1:20 **Chr.Ref.** 30
1:28 **SW** 143–4
2:15 **CLII** 193
3:2 **RP** 92
5:7–8 **FSE** 20
5:20–6:2 **PP** 89
6:3 **RP** 48
6:6 **FSE** 22
7 **Chr.Ref.** 106
7:18 **Chr.Ref.** 25, **FSE** 24
8:15 **LM** 33
8:16 **CLII** 940–1
8:18 **PP** 115, 122
8:19–23 **FSE** 90
8:19–22 **Dock** 20
8:20–1 **M** 70–1
8:20 **CLII** 747, **M** 155
8:21 **M** 139
8:22 **M** 124

11:22 **CLII** 804
12:2 **SW** 242
12:5 **WL** 412
12:20 **RP** 48
13:4 **EC** 292, **WL** 429
13:5 **SW** 193
13:8–10 **Chr.Ref.** 66, **FL** 105
13:14 **PP** 43, **MC** 160
13:20 **CLII** 903
14 **CLII** 285
14:4 **LM** 20
14:5 **SW** 143–4
15:4 **RP** 24

1 CORINTHIANS
GENERAL
CLII 62
1:20 **SW** 238
1:26 **CLII** 69, **Chr.Ref.** 30
2:6 **Chr.Ref.** 30
2:12 **SW** 233
2:14–15 **Toast** 85
2:16 **MC** 160, 186
3:4–6 **Chr.Reunion** 88
3:18 **Chr.Ref.** 30, **SW** 235
3:19 **SW** 238
3:22 **M** 139
3:23 **Chr.Ref.** 20 NB
    misprinted as '2:23'
4:4 **FST** 87, **SW** 187, 192
5:5 **PP** 71
6:3 **Toast** 100
6:13 **Toast** 108
6:16 **CLII** 394
7:5, 33–4 **FL** 89–90

7:10, 12 **WL** 479
7:25 **EC** 148, 151
7:31 **FL** 125
8 **CLII** 185
8:7 **SW** 192
8:10 **SW** 192
9:1 **M** 147 NB misprinted as
    'i.9'
9:16 **FSE** 105
10:1 **WL** 462
10:4 **WL** 456
10:13 **CLII** 869
10:27–31 **FSE** 31
10:31 **Chr.Ref.** 25, **LM** 25
11:1 **Chr.Ref.** 20
11:2–16 **CLII** 395–6
11:3, 7, 11, **Chr.Ref.** 19
11:24–5 **WL** 402, **LM** 132
11:24 **Dock** 26, 60
12 **WL** 402
12:1–11 **EC** 55
12:6 **FSE** 17
12:12–30 **PP** 120
13 **WL** 438
13:1 **WL** 455
13:4 **FL** 38
13:5 **FL** 122
13:7 **CLII** 863, **RP** 61
13:10 **Dock** 72–3
13:13 **WL** 425
14 **Chr.Ref.** 124, 126
14:18 **Toast** 85
14:20 **Chr.Ref.** 30, **MC** 70
15:6 **M** 148
15:20–28 **RP** 111